MIX
Papier aus verantwortungsvollen Quellen
Paper from responsible sources
FSC® C105338

Britta Tondock

How Self-Compassion can enhance Authentic Leadership Development

A quantitative study

Anchor Academic
Publishing

Tondock, Britta: How Self-Compassion can enhance Authentic Leadership Development: A quantitative study, Hamburg, Anchor Academic Publishing 2015

Buch-ISBN: 978-3-95489-379-9
PDF-eBook-ISBN: 978-3-8428-2285-6
Druck/Herstellung: Anchor Academic Publishing, Hamburg, 2015

Bibliografische Information der Deutschen Nationalbibliothek:
Die Deutsche Nationalbibliothek verzeichnet diese Publikation in der Deutschen Nationalbibliografie; detaillierte bibliografische Daten sind im Internet über http://dnb.d-nb.de abrufbar.

Bibliographical Information of the German National Library:
The German National Library lists this publication in the German National Bibliography. Detailed bibliographic data can be found at: http://dnb.d-nb.de

All rights reserved. This publication may not be reproduced, stored in a retrieval system or transmitted, in any form or by any means, electronic, mechanical, photocopying, recording or otherwise, without the prior permission of the publishers.

Das Werk einschließlich aller seiner Teile ist urheberrechtlich geschützt. Jede Verwertung außerhalb der Grenzen des Urheberrechtsgesetzes ist ohne Zustimmung des Verlages unzulässig und strafbar. Dies gilt insbesondere für Vervielfältigungen, Übersetzungen, Mikroverfilmungen und die Einspeicherung und Bearbeitung in elektronischen Systemen.

Die Wiedergabe von Gebrauchsnamen, Handelsnamen, Warenbezeichnungen usw. in diesem Werk berechtigt auch ohne besondere Kennzeichnung nicht zu der Annahme, dass solche Namen im Sinne der Warenzeichen- und Markenschutz-Gesetzgebung als frei zu betrachten wären und daher von jedermann benutzt werden dürften.

Die Informationen in diesem Werk wurden mit Sorgfalt erarbeitet. Dennoch können Fehler nicht vollständig ausgeschlossen werden und die Diplomica Verlag GmbH, die Autoren oder Übersetzer übernehmen keine juristische Verantwortung oder irgendeine Haftung für evtl. verbliebene fehlerhafte Angaben und deren Folgen.

Alle Rechte vorbehalten

© Anchor Academic Publishing, Imprint der Diplomica Verlag GmbH
Hermannstal 119k, 22119 Hamburg
http://www.diplomica-verlag.de, Hamburg 2015
Printed in Germany

Acknowledgements

The completion of this study would not have been possible without the constant support and valuable feedback of my supervisors professor Stephen Benton and Ayleen Wisudha from the University of Westminster, London. They always believed in my ideas and encouraged me to trust my instincts. My gratitude also goes to my friends and family, who guided me throughout the process with the never-ending belief that I would create great work.

I. Executive summary

In the face of today's business challenges, the demand for a more genuine leadership style is arising. Authentic Leadership as a way to authentically relate to oneself and others is meant to create meaning, trust and confidence amongst followers. At the same time, the Buddhist concept of Self-Compassion is becoming popular in the Western academic world. This study offers first insights into the relationship between Authentic Leadership and Self-Compassion. Theoretical similarities and connections between the two constructs are being presented. An online study (N=50) got conducted, asking young professionals from the international student organization 'AIESEC' about Authentic Leadership attributes and self-compassionate behaviours. Data analysis showed a weak positive correlation between Authentic Leadership and Self-Compassion. Methodical limitations of the study are being demonstrated. Implications for Authentic Leadership research and practice are being discussed, concluding that Self-Compassion could enhance the theoretical operationalization of authenticity as well as the intense process of Authentic Leadership Development.

This study was shortlisted for the Association of Business Psychologist's Workforce Experience Award in 2014.

II. Table of contents

I. Executive summary 5

1. Review of literature 9
1.1. Authentic Leadership 9
    1.1.1. Today's business world: In need of authenticity 9
    1.1.2. Characteristics of Authentic Leaders 10
    1.1.3. Positive impact of Authentic Leadership on followers 13
    1.1.4. Authentic Leadership and other leadership theories 14
1.2. Authentic Leadership and Self-Compassion 15
    1.2.1. Self-Compassion as a construct 15
    1.2.2. Self-Compassion and other self-related constructs in Authentic Leadership ... 17
        1.2.2.1. Self-Compassion and embracing vulnerability: accepting weakness 17
        1.2.2.2. Self-Compassion and self-esteem: intrinsic sense of worthiness 19
    1.2.3. Hypothetical impact of Self-Compassion on Authentic Leadership 20

2. Study design 24
2.1. Quantitative design 24
2.2. Population: the international student organization 'AIESEC' 24
2.3. Measurements 25
    2.3.1. Authentic Leadership Questionnaire (ALQ) 25
    2.3.2. Self-Compassion Scale (SCS) 26
2.4. Ethical considerations 26

3. Findings 28
3.1. Sample characteristics 28
3.2. Data distribution 28
3.3. Correlation between Self-Compassion and Authentic Leadership 29
3.4. Summary of findings 30

4. Discussion 32
4.1. Limitations 32
    4.1.1. Validity 32
        4.1.1.1. Validity of measurements: self-rating, social desirability and self-awareness of participants 32
        4.1.1.2. Statistical power of the study design: effect size, sample size and parametric test requirements 34
        4.1.1.3. Representativeness: AIESEC Alumni in the European Union 36
    4.1.2. Reliability of online measurements: internal and external disruptive variables 37
    4.1.4. Theoretical limitations of the study 37
4.2. Contributions 38
    4.2.1. Theoretical implications for Authentic Leadership: Self-Compassion as contributor to operationalize authenticity 38
    4.2.2. Practical implications for Authentic Leadership: Self-Compassion as major component for Authentic Leadership Development 41

5. Recommendations 44

III. References 47

IV. Appendices 51
IV.1. Ethics Approval Letter 51
IV.2. Overview of approached population 52
IV.3. Measurements 53
    IV.3.1. Questionnaire introduction 53
    IV.3.2. Demographic questions 54

- IV.3.3. Authentic Leadership Questionnaire – copyright 57
- IV.3.4. Authentic Leadership Questionnaire – online terms of use 59
- IV.3.5. Self-Compassion Scale 60
- IV.4. Sample characteristics 61
  - IV.4.1. Overview about demographic data 61
  - IV.4.2. Age distribution 64
  - IV.4.3. Geographic Region 65
  - IV.4.4. Educational background 65
  - IV.4.5. Number of team members 66
  - IV.4.6. Leadership experience in years 66
  - IV.4.7. Size of organization 67
  - IV.4.8. Occupational background 67
- IV.5. Statistical analysis 68
  - IV.5.1. Descriptive graphs 68
  - IV.5.2. Inferential analysis of the data 68
    - IV.5.2.1. Correlation: Self-Compassion and Authentic Leadership 68
    - IV.5.2.2. Correlation: Self-Kindness and Ethical/Moral 69
    - IV.5.2.3. Correlation: Self-Kindness and Balanced Processing 69
    - IV.5.2.4. Correlation: Common Humanity and Ethical/Moral 70
    - IV.5.2.5. Correlation: Common Humanity and Balanced Processing 70
    - IV.5.2.6. Correlation: Mindfulness and Ethical/Moral 71
    - IV.5.2.7. Correlation: Mindfulness and Balanced Processing 71
    - IV.5.2.8. Correlation: Self-Compassion and Ethical/Moral 72
    - IV.5.2.9. Correlation: Self-Compassion and Balanced Processing 72
    - IV.5.2.10. Correlation: Authentic Leadership and Common Humanity 73
    - IV.5.2.11. Correlation: Authentic Leadership and Mindfulness 73
  - IV.5.3. Correlations for different sub-groups 74
    - IV.5.3.1. Overview 74
    - IV.5.3.2. Male sample 74
    - IV.5.3.3. Female sample 75
    - IV.5.3.4. Age less than 30 years 75
    - IV.5.3.5. Age more than 30 years 76
    - IV.5.3.6. Active AIESECers 76
    - IV.5.3.7. Alumni 77
    - IV.5.3.8. Team size 2-12 people 77
    - IV.5.3.9. Team size over 12 people 78
    - IV.5.3.10. Less than 1 year of leadership experience 78
    - IV.5.3.11. 2-5 years of leadership experience 79
    - IV.5.3.12. Over 5 years of leadership experience 79
    - IV.5.3.13. Company size 1-100 people 80
    - IV.5.3.14. Company size over 100 people 80
    - IV.5.3.15. European Union 81
    - IV.5.3.16. South America 81
    - IV.5.3.17. Africa 82
    - IV.5.3.18. Asia 82
    - IV.5.3.19. Education & Training occupations 83
    - IV.5.3.20. Management occupations 83
    - IV.5.3.21. Business & Financial occupations 84

1. Review of literature

1.1. Authentic Leadership

1.1.1. Today's business world: In need of authenticity

> *'Collaborating with another human — especially a team of humans — is messy, deeply personal, profoundly meaningful stuff, and it should be treated as such. Personally speaking, if you're working with me, I know we've come together to do two things. One: Evolve as humans. Two: Make great stuff for the world. Sometimes it's unclear as to which is which, and I'm good with that'* (Danielle La Porte, 2013).

This charmingly candid quote by business coach and speaker Danielle LaPorte puts unequivocally into words what today's business world is in need of: a more human way of relating to each other, creating individual and organizational purpose. The challenges are numerous: the economic climate is characterized by never-known transformations such as new technologies, new market demands and global competition. Human beings in the workplace are faced with high levels of uncertainty and complexity. Job roles are becoming ambiguous, and change is a constant companion in organizations. Leaders who decide to look for their own advantage rather than taking the overall organizational well-being into consideration cause deep resignation and mistrust amongst employees and citizens (May et al., 2003). In this uncertain environment, a new demand for genuine leadership is arising. The lack of public trust in business and political leaders can have dangerous consequences for the privileges of our capitalistic system, which is why the development of leaders who treat people as the basis of their business success, not as another cost of doing business, is essential (George, 2007). People seek for meaning and connection in their daily working life, searching for leaders who can restore trust, confidence, hope, optimism and resilience. Today's society is in need of veritable and sustained performance based on ethical values that go beyond financial gains (Avolio & Gardner, 2005). People in organizations want to be trusted and take their part in the needed leadership:

> '[People in organizations] are demanding meaning and significance from their work, and are not willing to toil away just for someone else's benefit. They want to lead now, not wait in line for 10 to 20 years until they are tapped for a leadership role.' (George, 2007, p. 11).

The secret of leading tomorrow's organizations effectively therefore lies in the development of authentic leaders who can surround their employees amongst a common purpose, and who are equally able to facilitate their follower's authentic self-expression (Gardner et al., 2011).

1.1.2. Characteristics of Authentic Leaders

To begin with, we will describe in detail how authentic leaders can be characterized. Going back to the roots of authenticity as a concept, it firstly occurred in Greek philosophy as well as in the work of Heidegger and Sartre where the genuine development of self and others was central (Avolio & Gardner, 2005). It may also be influenced by the work of psychologists Carl Rogers and Maslow who focused on their research on self-actualized persons. Being true to oneself, expressing feelings, thoughts, emotions and beliefs autonomously and independently from those around us, was seen as core of developing an authentic self. In more recent research, becoming authentic is described as a transformative, life-long development process (George, 2007), and includes the following characteristics: developing an integrated self without playing a role, appreciating other's diversity and their right for personal development, influencing others via personal interaction and connection, challenging the context with the aim of self-expression, critical reflection about authenticity and the aim to support others in the development of their authenticity for the greater good (see Cranton & Carusetta, 2004, in the context of authentic teaching).

Coming from the perspective that a leader's authenticity emerges from his life story and how he makes sense of it, Shamir & Eilam (2005) define the clarity of a leaders self-concept, how the leader defines who he is, why and who he wants to become, as the core of authentic leadership. It includes that the leader sees his leadership role as a self-expressive act rather than a given position, that he has experienced his values to be true and uses them to guide his actions, that his goals are motivated by an internal commitment based on a personal cause and that he seeks for self-verification rather than admiration. W. George (2007), professor at Harvard Business School and former chairman and CEO, conducted one of the largest in-depth studies about how leaders develop, including interviews with 125 leaders from all areas and backgrounds. Congruent with the life-story approach of Shamir & Eilam (2005), the study revealed that what made those leaders successful came from earlier life experiences that created their mission. George (2007) describes the authentic self as who we are at our deepest level, where our satisfaction comes from, being our reference point in a rapidly changing world.

Based on the described internal and highly personal processes, several attempts to define common traits of an authentic leader personality have been made. A definition developed by Walumbwa et al. (2008) is both respected and used in the academic world to describe behavioural aspects of Authentic Leadership, which is why it will serve as the basis for this study. Walumbwa et al. (2008) suggest four traits to describe an authentic leader, measurable with the Authentic Leadership Questionnaire (ALQ):

a) **Self Awareness:** *To what degree is the leader aware of his or her strengths, limitations, how others see him or her and how the leader impacts others?*

Is the leader aware of his own vulnerabilities and deals with them openly, does he make them transparent and turn them into strength, making sure that everybody knows what or what not to expect from him? Self-awareness describes a continuous process where the individual gains insight into what constitutes their existence, such as unique talents, gifts, strengths, core beliefs, values, and desires (Avolio & Gardner, 2005).

b) **Transparency:** *To what degree does the leader reinforce a level of openness with others that provides them with an opportunity to be forthcoming with their ideas, challenges and opinions?*

Does the leader inspire others to action in modelling confidence, hope and resiliency? Does he "walk his talk"? Does he consistently build authenticity in his associates, helping them to build their psychological capacity and strength? Authentic follower development happens in a developmental process for both sides, relating to each other more and more authentically (Avolio & Gardner, 2005).

c) **Ethical/Moral:** *To what degree does the leader set a high standard for moral and ethical conduct?*

Does he show integrity between his personal values and those demonstrated in his working life? Is he guided by a set of values that follow what is right for his team or organization? May et al. (2003) describe that authentic leaders are those who own a heightened level of moral capacity: they acknowledge their role as including ethical responsibility and they recognize the intensity of moral situations.

d) **Balanced Processing:** *To what degree does the leader solicit sufficient opinions and viewpoints prior to making important decisions in order to be seen as fair and just?*

Is the leader able to judge issues and moral dilemmas from all angles without loosing credibility? Does he explore alternative ways of approaching moral dilemmas while still being seen to be acting consistent with his ultimate values and therefore authentic? Authentic leaders evaluate transparently all alternatives; they consider the possible consequences of their decision for all stakeholders and act with integrity based on their personal values and former experiences (May et al., 2003).

To summarize, the four common traits of an authentic leader are a high level of self-awareness about one's own identity and self, transparency about decisions and vulnerabilities and therefore authentic follower development, moral integrity aligning individual values with overall organizational well-being, and a balanced way to look at a moral dilemma considering the consequences for all stakeholders. Authentic leaders are said to be especially powerful in extreme or dangerous situations (Kolditz & Brazil, 2005), and authenticity is meant to have several positive outcomes on the leader's psychological health: studies found that authenticity is positively correlated with psychological well-being, self-acceptance, a sense of purpose and personal growth, and negatively correlated with contingent self-esteem, in which the individual self-worth depends upon meeting external measures and standards (Toor & Ofori, 2009; Kernis & Goldman, 2005).

1.1.3. Positive impact of Authentic Leadership on followers

The impact of authentic leaders on their followers has been positively outlined and explored by several authors. Numerous publications stated that Authentic Leadership behaviours lead to high personal and social identification with the leader (Avolio et al., 2004; Ilies et al., 2005) as well as to perceived behavioural integrity (Leroy et al., 2012). Those perceptions would positively impact follower's hope, trust and positive emotions (Avolio et al., 2004), follower's psychological capital, such as self-efficacy, optimism and resilience (Rego et al., 2012), behavioral modeling and increased self-determination (Ilies et al., 2005), and follower's organizational identification and stability in turbulent times (Leroy at al., 2012). As a result, this is meant to increase follower commitment, job satisfaction, meaningfulness, engagement, and job performance (Avolio et al, 2004); follower's expressiveness, self-realization, flow experiences and eudaemonic well-being (an intense state of self-expression and liveliness); self-efficacy and self-esteem (Ilies et al, 2005); and employee's creativity as a source for organizational innovation (Rego et al, 2012).

1.1.4. Authentic Leadership and other leadership theories

When comparing Authentic Leadership to other recent leadership theories, it has been labelled as a root construct for all forms of positive leadership, such as transformational, charismatic or spiritual leadership (Avolio & Gardner, 2005; May et al., 2003). Most similarities can be drawn to transformational leadership (Burns, 1978), such as being self-aware and open to personal development including a moral component to leadership. On the contrary, authentic leaders might not necessarily transform their followers into leaders themselves, but rather nurture a community of followers who belief in the purpose of their organization. Compared to charismatic leadership, where impression management plays an important role, an authentic leader rather leads by creating meaning and connection for themselves and others. In spiritual leadership, no clear empiric research background is evident, whereas Authentic Leadership research draws from clinic, positive and social psychology (Avolio & Gardner, 2005).

> *'Authentic leaders are not necessarily transformational, visionary, or charismatic leaders. They don't stand out every day. But these are the leaders who, when called upon by the hand of fate, will be the ones who take a stand that changes the course of history for others, be they organizations, departments or just other individuals.'* (May et al., 2003, p. 248).

It seems that Authentic Leadership adds a deeper layer to leadership research, as it does not primarily describe traits or contents of values of a leader, but rather a way of being in one's leadership in an authentic and deeply self-fulfilling way (Shamir & Eilam, 2005).

1.2. Authentic Leadership and Self-Compassion

After having given a short overview about current needs for Authentic Leadership, characteristics of authentic leaders, authentic leaders' impact on followers and a brief orientation in the context of other leadership theories, we will now focus on the self-related qualities that underlie Authentic Leadership. As mentioned by several authors in the field, the development of authenticity and therefore authentic leadership is a very intense, highly personal and life-long developmental process, as it involves all parts of one's being - including personal weaknesses, vulnerabilities, and confronting painful experiences from one's past (see Shamir & Eilam, 2005). It takes immense courage and daily practice to fully embrace and acknowledge one's authentic self with both flaws and natural talents.

Still, there is little agreement on the core constructs and underlying psychological processes responsible for the increased authenticity of a leader. This study attempts to increase the understanding and development of authenticity and authentic leadership behaviours in bringing a new concept into Authentic Leadership research: the construct of Self-Compassion. The art of being compassionate towards oneself could be a fundamental part of becoming authentic. The following paragraph will outline why and how the two constructs could be connected.

1.2.1. Self-Compassion as a construct

The concept of Self-Compassion stems from Buddhist philosophy and is relatively new in the Western psychology. It describes an alternative and less egocentric approach for developing a healthy relationship towards oneself. It is likely to be related to self-empathy, humanistic psychology and emotional development. Due to Neff (2003a), the construct is understood and defined using three sub-variables:

1. *Self-Kindness:* extending kindness and understanding to oneself rather than harsh self-criticism and judgment

2. *Common Humanity:* seeing one's experiences as part of the larger human experience rather than as separating and isolating
3. *Mindfulness:* holding one's painful thoughts and feelings in balanced awareness rather than over-identifying with them.

Self-compassion includes the assumption that one's suffering, failure and inadequacies are part of the human condition and that all people, including oneself, are worthy of compassion:

> *'Self-compassion, therefore, involves being touched by and open to one's own suffering, not avoiding or disconnecting from it, generating the desire to alleviate one's suffering and to heal oneself with kindness. Self-compassion also involves offering non-judgmental understanding to one's pain, inadequacies and failures, so that one's experience is seen as part of the larger human experience'* (Neff, 2003a, p. 87).

Self-Compassion can be a powerful force for individual growth and change, as it creates the emotional safety needed to see oneself clearly without the fear of harmful self-judgment. It protects against self-evaluative anxiety when faced with personal weaknesses (Neff et al., 2007a). Further studies found that Self-Compassion moderates individual's reactions to unpleasant life events, such as failure, rejection or embarrassment: people with high levels of Self-Compassion showed lower negative emotions, accepted responsibility for their role in negative events and were generally more willing to accept undesirable aspects of their character. Additionally, it has been hypothesized that Self-Compassion functions as a buffer for negative life events, as individuals are able to make more accurate self-evaluations without self-criticism or defensive self-enhancement (Leary et al., 2007). Positive correlations have been found between Self-Compassion and positive psychological functioning (such as happiness, optimism, wisdom or curiosity) as well as the big-five personality traits agreeableness, extroversion and conscientiousness (Neff et al., 2007b).

Due to its non-judgmental nature, Self-Compassion is meant to protect against narcissism, self-centeredness, social comparison as well as self-criticism, feelings of isolation, depression and anxiety. It is likely to foster proactive behaviors restoring and maintaining mental well-being, psychological health and life satisfaction (Neff, 2003a).

1.2.2. Self-Compassion and other self-related constructs in Authentic Leadership

The non-judgmental nature of Self-Compassion is a unique trait that could be central for the development of self-expressed and authentic being in one's leadership role. Taking a close look at the concept of Self-Compassion with its three variables Self-Kindness, Common Humanity and Mindfulness, remarkable similarities to other self-related concepts in the context of Authentic Leadership become evident. A simple theoretical model showing Self-Compassion as a root construct for Authentic Leadership is being developed in the following.

1.2.2.1. Self-Compassion and embracing vulnerability: accepting weakness

First of all, Self-Compassion connects closely to the work about vulnerability and authenticity by social work professor Dr. Brene Brown (PhD). Brown (2010) defines authenticity as *'...the daily practice of letting go of who we think we're supposed to be and embracing who we are'* (Brown, 2010, p.50). It seems that in order to do so, one would need a high level of *'Self-Kindness':* to extend kindness and understanding to oneself rather than self-criticism and judgment (Neff, 2003a). Brown (2010) further on writes that authentic living and leading would include to cultivate the courage to be imperfect and to fully accept one's vulnerabilities as part of being human – which seems to be an equivalent of the variable *'Common Humanity':* seeing one's experience as part of the larger human experience rather than isolating (Neff, 2003a).

Diddams & Chang (2012) support this connection in stating that the full acceptance of weakness lays at the core of authenticity. Referring to the four characteristics of Authentic Leadership (Walumbwa et al., 2008), namely *Self-Awareness, Transparency, Ethical/Moral* and *Balanced Processing*, they state how important it is for Authentic Leadership development to accept weaknesses in all four areas: The acknowledgement of never being able to know everything about oneself (*Self-Awareness*), the acceptance of occasional non-congruence between attitudes and behaviours (*Balanced Processing*), modesty about own moral judgments (*Moral/Ethical*) and generous openness not only about failures, but also flaws and fears (*Transparency*) would lead to greater authenticity than otherwise. This shows similarities to the variable *'Self-Kindness'* (being kind towards every aspect of one's being, including unflattering ones) and interprets the variable *'Common Humanity'* accurately:

> *'We advocate for a conception of self-esteem that is not only strong enough to avoid this defensiveness when confronted with negative feedback but includes the continual presence of weakness as part of its self-schemata. [...] We suggest that leaders' acceptance of their weaknesses as authentic is not only developmentally appropriate but in being only human, frees them to unselve and create greater good among their followers.'*

(Diddams & Chang, 2012, p. 600)

Considering that both *'Self-Kindness'* and *'Common Humanity'* may lie at the core of accepting one's vulnerabilities, it is interesting to see what Brown (2012) concludes about vulnerability in the context of Authentic Leadership: *'To reignite creativity, innovation, and learning, leaders must re-humanize education and work. This means understanding how scarcity is affecting the way we lead and work, [and] learning how to engage with vulnerability [...]'* (Brown, 2012, p. 184). It brings the perspective to our work life that leaders must recognize human beings as the essence of organizations, including themselves. Dealing with human beings is a vulnerable process which, when being acknowledged as such, will lead to constant engagement and growth:

'If you want a culture of creativity and innovation where sensible risks are embraced on both a market and individual level, start by developing the ability of managers to cultivate an openness to vulnerability in their teams. And this, paradoxically perhaps, requires first that they are vulnerable themselves. This notion that the leader needs to be 'in charge' and to 'know all the answers' is both dated and destructive.'

Peter Sheahan, CEO of ChangeLabs ™, cited in Brown (2012), p.65.

Based on this connection, practicing Self-Compassion could support leaders in embracing their vulnerabilities and becoming more authentic. It could make an important contribution to re-humanize work, to reignite creativity and to re-create meaning for their organizations.

1.2.2.2. Self-Compassion and self-esteem: intrinsic sense of worthiness

The conceptualization of self-esteem by Kernis (2003) has heavily influenced the genesis of Authentic Leadership, and interestingly enough similarities between an optimal sense of self-esteem and Self-Compassion can be found. Especially the variables *'Self-Kindness'* and *'Mindfulness'* seem to relate to what Kernis (2003) defines an optimal sense of self-esteem: it includes well-anchored and secure feelings of self-worth shown by *'...people who like, value, and accept themselves, imperfections and all' (p.3)*. This unconditional acceptance of oneself goes along with the description of *'Self-Kindness'* and might be a consequence of showing kind understanding towards oneself. Kernis (2003) further on mentions that people with secure high self-esteem do not compare their worthiness to others, and their feelings of self-worth are not easily challenged: negative feedback or poor performance might lead to the conclusion of not being good at a particular task, but it does not affect their overall sense of worthiness (also see Diddams & Chang, 2012). It could be that this capacity is a result of showing *'Mindfulness'*: holding one's painful thoughts and feelings in balanced awareness rather than over-identifying with them (Neff, 2003a). If an individual does not over identify with unpleasant self-related information, it might be that unflattering facts can be accepted peacefully and without self-destructing consequences. Concerning the benefits of optimal self-esteem, Kernis (2003) concludes that a strong sense of intrinsic worthiness and the acknowledgement of weakness is likely to increase a leader's authenticity: *'Authenticity can be characterized as reflecting the unobstructed operation of one's true, or core, self in one's daily enterprise'* (Kernis, 2003, p.13).

Showing Self-Compassion towards oneself could be equivalent to the development of an optimal sense of self-esteem. Studies showed that Self-Compassion was moderately correlated with self-esteem (Neff, 2003b), and yet the correlation was low enough to assume that both constructs can be discriminated from each other. For example, Self-Compassion did not have significant correlations with narcissism, whereas self-esteem did. Other research comparing high self-esteem with Self-Compassion found that Self-Compassion is more predictive of caring and supportive relationship behavior than self-esteem (Neff & Beretvas, 2013), and some even consider Self-Compassion as a possible alternative to self-esteem for developing a healthy sense of worthiness (Neff & Vonk, 2009). Contradictory to Kernis' (2003) definition of optimal self-esteem, the original construct of self-esteem is often associated with a high level of positive self-evaluations about oneself, which includes external comparison to others. High self-esteem therefore might have more downsides to psychological health than the non-evaluative nature of Self-Compassion (Neff, 2011).

1.2.3. Hypothetical impact of Self-Compassion on Authentic Leadership

To summarize, a review of the literature showed that Self-Compassion with its three sub-variables contains interesting similarities to the theory of vulnerability and optimal self-esteem in the context of authenticity. As outlined, Self-Compassion could support a leader in kindly embracing his vulnerabilities, developing a healthy sense of authenticity. Furthermore, Self-Compassion could be equivalent or contributing to the development of optimal, intrinsic self-esteem. Both an optimal sense of self-esteem as well as the acceptance of personal vulnerabilities is described as crucial for the development of authenticity (Kernis, 2003; Brown, 2010; Diddams & Chang, 2012), which consequently determines how authentic an individual behaves in a leadership role. Given that our analysis has some truth in it, Self-Compassion should support the development of the four qualities of Authentic Leaders described by Walumbwa et al. (2008). The following model gives an overview about the made connections.

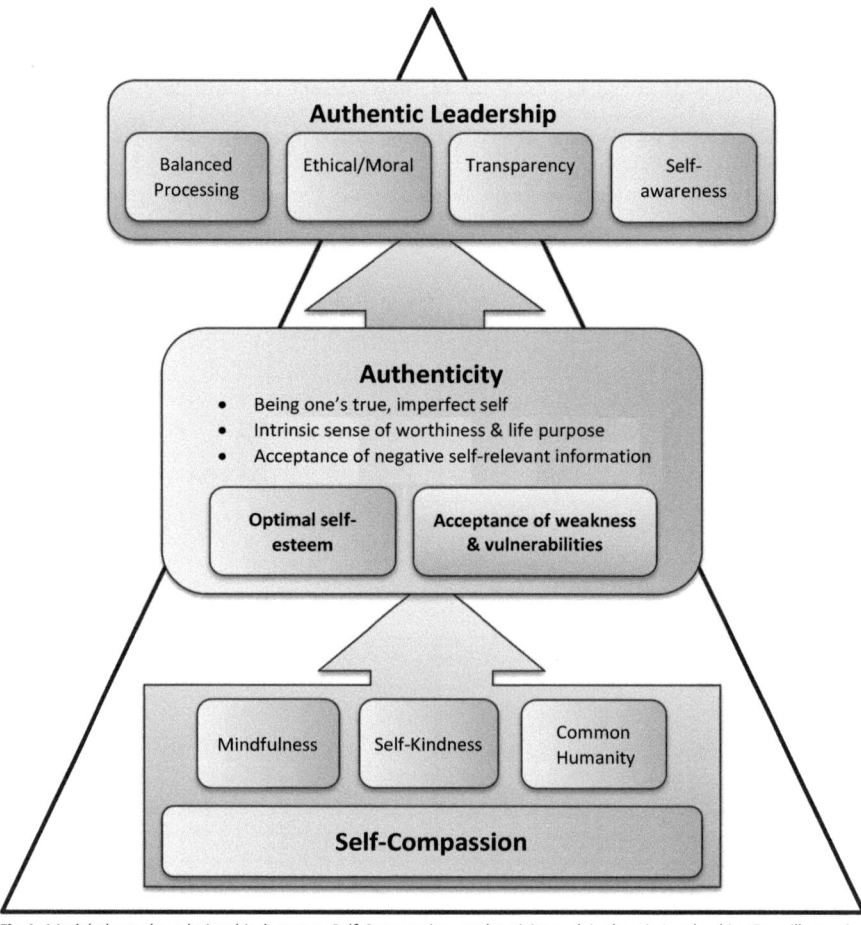

Fig.1: *Model about the relationship between Self-Compassion, authenticity and Authentic Leadership. Own illustration based on Neff (2003a), Kernis (2003), Walumbwa et al. (2008), Brown (2010) and Diddams & Chang (2012).*

While several authors consider Authentic Leadership as the root construct for other positive forms of leadership (Avolio & Gardner, 2005; Shamir & Eilam, 2005), we might assume based on our investigations that Self-Compassion could be a root construct for authenticity and Authentic Leadership. The developed model in analogy to the 'iceberg model' (first introduced by Hall, 1967) shows that the core of Authentic Leadership could lie in the practice of Self-Compassion. Whereas the behaviours of an authentic leader are visible at the top of the iceberg, the larger portion of Authentic Leadership lies beneath the surface. The development of authenticity, including the psychological capacity to practice Self-Compassion, is an underlying and intensely personal process not observable at first sight.

Although our model cannot provide sound hypothesis about direct relationships between the three variables of Self-Compassion and the four distinct characteristics of authentic leaders, we could formulate expectations about possible correlations: *'Self-Kindness'* might contribute to *'Self-Awareness'*, as embracing instead of criticizing one's flaw's is necessary to become aware of weaknesses, dealing with them openly. A sense of *'Common Humanity'* could be needed to develop strong *'Ethical/Moral'* values and to recognize one's ethical responsibility for the whole organization. Lastly, *'Mindfulness'* with one's thoughts and feelings could be both valuable to develop a healthy sense of *'Self-Awareness'* as well as *'Balanced Processing'*: who does not run away or over-identify with painful thoughts and feelings might be more eager to see one's inadequacies clearly and to carefully as well as transparently evaluate different alternatives for a decision.

In case Self-Compassion would be a core construct for Authentic Leadership, new horizons and opportunities for Authentic Leadership Development would arise. The following study was conducted with the aim to find first empirical evidence for this relationship, guided by the research question: Does Self-Compassion increase the authenticity of a leader?

2. Study design

2.1. Quantitative design

Given the fact that validated quantitative measurements for both constructs already exist, it seemed logical to use those existing questionnaires for a first exploration of the field, therefore choosing a quantitative study design. Based on the review of the literature, we assume that a high level of Self-Compassion would result in a high level of a leader's authenticity. Therefore, the hypothesis we want to maintain is the following (H1):

- *H1: There is a positive correlation between a leader's level of Self-Compassion (SC) and his level of authenticity (AL).*

Accordingly, the hypothesis we would like to falsify is the following (H0):

- *H0: There is no correlation between a leader's level of Self-Compassion (SC) and his level of authenticity (AL).*

As we are making both a prediction about the presence of a significant effect and the direction of this effect, our hypothesis is one-tailed (Brace et al., 2006). Considering the direction of our research question, Self-Compassion would be the independent, Authentic Leadership the dependent variable.

2.2. Population: the international student organization 'AIESEC'

The population for this sample consists of young students and professionals involved with the international student organization 'AIESEC'. AIESEC is an independent, non-political, non-for-profit organization run by students and graduates of higher education. The organization is delivering leadership activities as well as international internship experiences for 86.000 members in 124 countries, and has been doing so for more than 60 years (see AIESEC website, 2013a). Participants got approached via the professional online communities 'LinkedIn' and 'XING Germany', as members of the organization are present in large numbers and organized in succinct groups on both platforms. Both active members and Alumni were considered *(for a detailed overview about the approached groups, see IV.2. in appendices)*. The online questionnaire was designed using the survey software *Qualtrics*. It got posted weekly over a timely period of seven weeks.

2.3. Measurements

The two variables Authentic Leadership and Self-Compassion got operationalized using existing sub-scales and measured with two existing questionnaires. For this study, the two questionnaires got combined. The final measurement therefore consisted of 42 items and 9 demographic questions being answered via self-rating of the participants *(for a detailed version of the questionnaire, see IV.3. in appendices)*. The structure of the used measurements shall be described in the following.

2.3.1. Authentic Leadership Questionnaire (ALQ)

The construct Authentic Leadership (AL) got measured with the Authentic Leadership Questionnaire (ALQ) developed by Walumbwa et al (2008). It is a theory-driven leadership survey designed to measure the four components that have been conceptualized as defining Authentic Leadership, namely *Self Awareness*, *Transparency*, *Ethical/Moral* and *Balanced Processing*. The original questionnaire includes a self-rating and an external rating by peers, whereas in this study only the self-rating part was used. It consists of 16 items, for example 'As a leader I say exactly what I mean' *(Transparency)*, 'I demonstrate beliefs that are consistent with actions' *(Ethical/Moral)*, or 'I seek feedback to improve interactions with others' *(Self-Awareness)*, rated on a Likert Scale from 1 (*Not at all*) to 5 (*Frequently, if not always*). Copyright for this questionnaire is held by Avolio, Gardner & Walumbwa (2007), and permission to use the questionnaire for this study has been granted *(delivered by Mind Garden, see IV.3.3. in appendices)*.

2.3.2. Self-Compassion Scale (SCS)

Following the 16 items of the ALQ, the questionnaire continued with 26 self-rated items measuring the construct Self-Compassion, taken in its original form following the Self-Compassion Scale developed by Neff (2003) *(find the complete questionnaire in IV.3.5. in appendices)*. The items measure the three sub-scales of Self-Compassion including their negative counterpart, namely *Self-Kindness* (Self-Judgment), *Common Humanity* (Isolation) and *Mindfulness* (Over-Identification). Participants rated themselves on a Likert-Scale from 1 (*Almost Never*) to 5 (*Almost Always*) on items such as 'I try to be loving towards myself when I'm feeling emotional pain' *(Self-Kindness)*, 'When things are going badly for me, I see the difficulties as part of life that everyone goes through' *(Common Humanity)* or 'When something upsets me I try to keep my emotions in balance' *(Mindfulness)*. For data analysis and calculation of overall sub-scales, scores for the negative sub-scales (Self-Judgment, Isolation and Over-Identification) got reversed.

2.4. Ethical considerations

The design and administration of the questionnaire complies with the BPS "Guidelines for Minimum Standards of Ethical Approval in Psychological Research" and the BPS "Ethical Principles for Conducting Research with Human Participants". The study got approved by the Psychology Ethics Committee *(see Ethics Approval Letter, IV.1. in appendices)*. Criterion to participate in the study was a minimum age of 18 years and to be or have been in a leadership position. Before starting the questionnaire, the participants got asked to give their consent that their participation is voluntarily, that their data would be collected anonymously and that they could withdraw their data from the study at any time. Due to ethical concerns, the Authentic Leadership Questionnaire did not include any external rating from peers or subordinates, as we did not want to give the impression that participation in the study would be tied to further conditions collecting sensible external data. Each measurement used in the questionnaire stayed in its original form, using the exact same items in the same order to guarantee validity and to respect copyright for the online use of the ALQ *(see IV.3.4. in appendices)*. It was also respected that only three sample items from the ALQ may be reproduced, and that the entire instrument may not be included or reproduced at any time in any other published material.

3. Findings

3.1. Sample characteristics

The overall sample consisted of N=50 with equal distribution in gender (50% male, 50% female). The majority of the participants were between 18 and 30 years old (70%), most of them were Alumni of the organization (84%) and the most common time frame for leadership experiences was either less than one year (40%) or between 2 and 5 years (50%). They are or were leading small or medium sized teams with 2-12 members (68%) in either small and medium sized companies up to 100 employees (58%) or large organizations with more than 1.000 employees (24%). Most of them are currently working in the European Union (72%) with some participants from South America (10%), Asia (6%) and Africa (4%). The majority (76%) owns a degree of higher education (48% Master's, 28% Bachelor's) and their occupational background focuses on Education & Training (30%), Management (16%), Business & Finance (10%) or Sales (8%). For detailed figures about the demographic data see IV.4. in appendices.

3.2. Data distribution

On average, the test scores for Self-Compassion (SC, 26 items) were higher than those for Authentic Leadership (AL, 16 items), but also more scattered: The mean for SC lay at 89.24 points with a Standard Deviation (SD) of ± 14.14, whereas the mean for AL lay at 65.62 points with a SD of ± 5.53. The following scatter-gram gives an overview about the overall distribution of the data along the regression line. No obvious abnormal data sets or freak values could be identified.

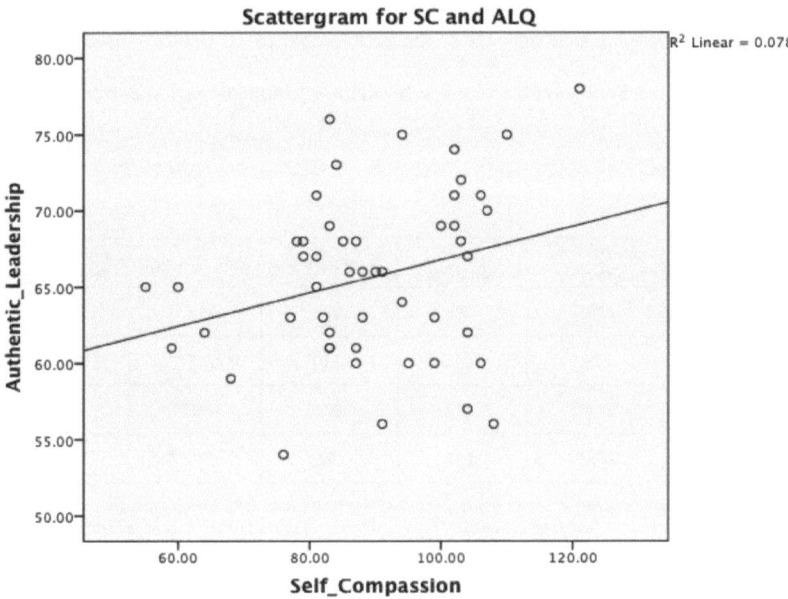

Fig. 2: Scatter-gram for the distribution of data sets of Self-Compassion (SC, on x-axis) and Authentic Leadership (AL, on y-axis).

3.3. Correlation between Self-Compassion and Authentic Leadership

For inferential analysis, Pearson's Correlation (r) got chosen as a parametric statistical test: our level of measurement can be considered interval (Likert-Scale) and we wanted to know about the degree or strength of the relationship between the two variables Self-Compassion (SC) and Authentic Leadership (AL). Due to our one-tailed hypothesis (H1), we assumed that there would be a positive correlation between SC and AL: the higher the level of SC, the higher the level of AL would be. Pearson's Correlation (r) ranges from -1 (perfect negative correlation) over 0 (no correlation) to +1 (perfect positive correlation). The analysis revealed a weak positive correlation between SC and AL (r=.279*, N=50, p<.05, one-tailed).

The following table shows further correlations between the sub-variables of SC and AL. The correlations between SC and two sub-variables of AL, *Ethical/Moral* (r=.356**, p<.01, one-tailed) and *Balanced Processing* (r=.335**, p<.01, one-tailed), were moderate and significant at the 0.01-level, meaning that only 1% of the data happened by chance. There were no significant correlations between SC and the sub-variables *Self-Awareness* and *Transparency* (between r=-.013 and .137).

Pearson's r (one-tailed)	Authentic Leadership	Self-Awareness	Transparency	Ethical/Moral	Balanced Processing
Self-Compassion	*.279**	.084	.096	*.356***	*.335***
Self-Kindness	.229	-.013	.110	.335**	.289*
Common Humanity	.249*	.137	.075	.282*	.271*
Mindfulness	.266*	.101	.069	.330**	.335**

Fig. 3: Pearson's r correlations between Self-Compassion and Authentic Leadership including sub-scales.
*. Correlation is significant at the 0.05 level (1-tailed). **. Correlation is significant at the 0.01 level (1-tailed).

Comparing the strength of correlation in different sub-groups of the sample, the correlation seemed to be slightly stronger for participants aged 30 years or younger (r=.300*, N=35). Furthermore, the correlation was stronger for participants leading a smaller team with 12 people or less (r=.326*, N=34) and for those working for a bigger company with more than 100 people (r=.414*, N=21). There was no difference in significance concerning the correlations for male and female participants, as well as for participants with longer or shorter leadership experiences. For a detailed overview about different sample groups, and correlations, see IV.5.3. in appendices.

3.4. Summary of findings

Our analysis revealed a statistically significant correlation (r=.279*, N=50, p<.05) between Self-Compassion and Authentic Leadership, measured with a self-rating online questionnaire. In this context, we can therefore accept our hypothesis (H1) saying that there would be a positive correlation between the two variables, and reject the null-hypothesis (H0) that there wouldn't. The correlation was especially moderate for participants aged less than 30 years, leading or having lead smaller teams with less than 13 people and working for larger organizations with over 1.000 employees. We can further on say that Self-Compassion correlated moderately and slightly stronger with two sub-constructs of Authentic Leadership, *Ethical/Moral* and *Balanced Processing*.

4. Discussion

4.1. Limitations

Although this study found a positive correlation between the questionnaire scores of Self-Compassion and Authentic Leadership, several limitations need to be discussed.

4.1.1. Validity

4.1.1.1. Validity of measurements: self-rating, social desirability and self-awareness of participants

When it comes to the used measurements, we can say that existing validation studies concluded a sufficient level of validity. The used Self-Compassion-Scale (SCS) by Neff (2003b) with validation studies of N=391 and N=232 revealed sound psychometric properties and theoretical validity, showing high internal consistency (Cronbach's Alpha = .92) and good construct validity. The Authentic Leadership Questionnaire (ALQ) by Walumbwa et al. (2008) represents a theory-based measure with satisfying internal consistency (Cronbach's Alpha between .72 and .92), construct validity, reliability as well as potential cross-cultural validity, having accessed a large sample size from China (N=212), Kenya (=478), and the US (N=224, N= 178, N= 236). Results show that Authentic Leadership can be discriminated from other leadership forms, such as ethical leadership and transformational leadership, and that self-rating reports correlated with external ratings from supervisors.

Although the two measurements showed sound parametric characteristics separate from each other, we need to consider the possible consequences of combining both questionnaires for our study in an online setting. Participants knew that the study would focus on Authentic Leadership and Self-Compassion *(see introduction text, IV.3.1. in appendices)*, but as the two parts of the questionnaire were not clearly separated from each other, it might have been confusing for some. The Authentic Leadership Questionnaire (ALQ) contains items that ask specific questions about individual behaviour as a leader *('As a leader, I...')*, whereas the Self-Compassion Scale (SCS) refers to individual behaviour and thought patterns in difficult times

('How I typically act towards myself in difficult times'). As there was no clear separation inside the questionnaire between the ALQ and the SCS without separated instructions for the SCS, some participants might still have answered the SCS with the mind-set of being asked about their leadership behaviour. They also might not have been aware of the fact that the SCS items especially referred to painful or unflattering personal experiences. We therefore cannot be sure if the used questionnaires measured the original constructs that they were supposed to measure. For further studies exploring the relationship between Authentic Leadership and Self-Compassion, it would be strongly advisable to give concise and clear instructions before starting each part of the questionnaire in order to set the right scene regarding the underlying context of the measurements.

Additionally, the disruptive variable of social desirability, meaning that participants answer based on what they think people want to hear, rather than on their own opinion or behaviour, may have invalidated several responses. On the other hand, it has also been found that social desirability and social anxiety were lower in anonymous online-questionnaires compared to pen and paper settings (Joinson, 1999). The used online-method might therefore still represent more valid results than other available settings.

Connected to this, the level of self-awareness of participants was a major factor in our study for the data to be valid, as it contained personal questions about leadership style and behaviour in difficult times. Looking at the characteristics of the sample, we could assume that participants were able to answer in congruence with their behaviours, as people having been involved with the student organization AIESEC usually do have an increased sense of self-awareness and self-concept clarity. The organization focuses on leadership development and intercultural exchange; therefore the amount of personal growth and learning resulting from challenges that involve living in a foreign culture or leading a group of people can be tremendous (see AIESEC, 2013b). Nevertheless, we need to consider that we will never be able to know everything about ourselves (see Diddams & Chang, 2012), and that even if the answers to the questions were given genuinely and with best intentions, it still might be that participants weren't aware of eventual blind spots or unconscious behaviours.

The phenomenon of social desirability could also have an even higher influence in the context of AIESEC, where self-reflection and personal growth is valued, but also expected: it could be that several participants answered from a place where they knew that certain behaviours as a leader or individual are desirable, and they therefore gave themselves a higher score, but in reality they did not reach the point to actually display those behaviours yet. Therefore, an external rating from boss, peer groups or subordinates would have brought light to those eventual blind spot's, given deeper insight into the validity of the study results and expanded the perception of participants concerning their personal development.

4.1.1.2. Statistical power of the study design: effect size, sample size and parametric test requirements

Considering the statistical power of our measurements, we need to answer the question if it really measured the existing correlation between Authentic Leadership (AL) and Self-Compassion (SC) in reality. The design of this study revealed certain limitations in terms of validity, considering the solely self-rating of participants and therefore a possible gap between internal perception and actual behaviour, and certain inaccuracies in the set-up of combining two questionnaires into one. However, our study showed a significant positive correlation between AL and SC with a sample size of only N=50, and we can expect the effect size to be bigger when testing a larger sample (Brace et al., 2006). Additionally, parametric tests do have certain statistical power, as they are able to calculate probabilities about the existence of an effect in reality, giving the probability (p-value) of either 5% ($p<.05$) or 1% ($p<.01$) that the found correlation happened by chance. Looking at the data requirements to carry out a parametric test, our data meets most of them: the data collected needs to have interval scale (Likert-Scale), the data should be normally distributed *(see IV.5.1. in appendices)*, and the compared samples should have equal variance.

This last requirement might be the one not fully given for the data in this study: the scores for Self-Compassion are more scattered than those for Authentic Leadership (SC: SD=±14.14, AL: SD=±5.53), which makes a difference in variance of 169.36 (Variance for SC=199.94, AL=30.58). We can therefore say that the scores for SC had a bigger influence on the results than the scores for AL, as the individual data sets for SC are more out of proportion. Considering our study design and the combination of two different, existing measurements with a different number of items, this is comprehensible: The construct of Authentic Leadership (AL) got measured using only 16 items, whereas Self-Compassion (SC) got measured with 26 items. It appears natural that participants score with a higher variance in their answers if they have more possibilities (items) to do so.

Additionally, the mean score for Self-Compassion was higher than the one for Authentic Leadership (SC: M=89.24, AL: M=65.62). The different ways of measurement concerning the sub-variables of the two constructs may have influenced this: Whereas Authentic Leadership got measured with items belonging to the four distinct sub-factors *Self-Awareness, Transparency, Balanced Processing* and *Ethical/Moral,* Self-Compassion was measured using six distinct sub-scales, consisting of three pairs representing positive and negative counterparts of Self-Compassion: *Self-Kindness* and *Self-Judgment, Mindfulness* and *Over-Identification, Common Humanity* and *Isolation*. For data analysis, the scores for the negative qualities (*Self-Judgment, Over-Identification* and *Isolation*) got reversed and the overall mean for *Self-Kindness, Mindfulness* and *Common Humanity* got calculated. Considering that human beings might easily reject negative behaviours about themselves, but not as likely accept very positive self-related attributes, the higher scores for SC could also result from the likelihood to answer a question about negative self-relevant information with a stronger tendency to say 'Not at all', therefore resulting in lower values, whereas the same item, formulated in a very positive way, would have gotten a less stronger response. As the possibly very low item scores containing negative self-relevant information got reversed for data analysis, we might have therefore gotten a higher overall score for Self-Compassion than we would have in case the items measuring negative sub-scales would have asked for the same qualities, but referring to very positive self-relevant information.

To conclude, the statistical power of our measurement can be evaluated as medium. The used measurements showed sufficient validity and reliability in validation studies, although dishonest or unconscious answers due to the self-rating must be considered. Additionally, the difference in variance of Self-Compassion and Authentic Leadership as well as different calculation of test scores impacted the results. Still our study gives a first sense about the possible correlation between Self-Compassion and Authentic Leadership in reality. Studies using concise measurements and larger samples are likely to achieve a bigger effect size.

4.1.1.3. Representativeness: AIESEC Alumni in the European Union

Answering the question if our sample is representative for the whole population, we cannot refer to existing data: demographical statistics about membership data of AIESEC are unfortunately not accessible to the public. Still, based on the characteristics of the organization, we can expect with some probability that our sample represents the average AIESEC Alumni in most areas: they are young professionals between 18 and 30 years old, having had a respectable amount of leadership experience, owning a degree of higher education and working in either Education & Training, Management, Business & Financial or Sales. Further on, our sample included individuals of AIESEC who are eager and willing to participate in an online questionnaire and who are active in the approached online communities, where a certain level of internet-affinity and openness could be suspected. All of those characteristics could be appropriate to describe the majority of former participants of the organization. One aspect that may not be fully representative for AIESEC Alumni is that our sample mainly consisted of participants currently resident in the European Union. A bigger range of participants from all over the world would have represented the different cultural backgrounds of members in AIESEC in a better way.

4.1.2. Reliability of online measurements: internal and external disruptive variables

In terms of reliability, we have to consider a set of disruptive variables influencing the results of the online questionnaire and therefore eventual differences in results when testing the same sample again. First, there might have been external conditions that disrupted participants while filling out the questionnaire and therefore influenced the validity of the data, such as a noisy surrounding, interruption through colleagues or friends, being in a rush, doing it parallel to different activities or eventual technical problems. Second, internal factors, such as the participant's mood or his current psychological condition, may have impacted his level of concentration, self-awareness or the willingness to answer honestly. Another factor to consider is that English might not have been first language for the majority of participants. Eventual misunderstandings or translation difficulties could have influenced data reliability.

4.1.4. Theoretical limitations of the study

To summarize the discussion of psychometrical limitations, we need to consider the influence of external environment, internal psychological states, social desirability, unawareness of emotional patterns or missing integrity between attitudes and behaviours for validity of study results. An external rating could have brought light into potential blind spots of the participants. However, the used design can be considered to have medium statistical power, and studies with a bigger sample size would be advisable. Lastly, the study is likely to be representative for young professionals with background in AIESEC and high activity on professional online communities.

In theoretical terms, we also need to emphasize that the found correlation does not indicate a causal relationship: for our study, we cannot say if Self-Compassion increased the authenticity of a leader or if Authentic Leadership behaviours caused a high level of Self-Compassion. Considering our original research question, asking if Self-Compassion would increase the authenticity of a leader, hence assuming a specific direction of the relationship, the chosen study design was not suitable to give a clear answer. Operationalizing Self-Compassion as the independent variable, and comparing a group of highly self-compassionate individuals to a randomized control group with regards to their level of authenticity, would have been an appropriate design to fit the formulation of the research question.

4.2. Contributions

Apart from the discussed limitations, this study showed that Self-Compassion is related to Authentic Leadership and that it is therefore worth exploring in the context of Authentic Leadership research and practice. Self-Compassion could be a contributing factor to the development of authenticity and Authentic Leadership behaviours.

4.2.1. Theoretical implications for Authentic Leadership: Self-Compassion as contributor to operationalize authenticity

Based on the study results, Self-Compassion could especially contribute to the development of Authentic Leadership characteristics *Ethical/Moral* and *Balanced Processing*. Before conducting our study, several expectations about the detailed correlations between sub-constructs of Self-Compassion and Authentic Leadership were made *(see chapter 1.2.3.)*. We expected that *'Self-Kindness'* would correlate with *'Self-Awareness'*, we hypothesized that *'Common Humanity'* could be correlated with *'Ethical/Moral'*, and that *'Mindfulness'* could be correlated with *'Self-Awareness'* as well as *'Balanced Processing'*. Looking at the results, our expectations got partly fulfilled: all three sub-constructs of Self-Compassion correlated significantly ($p<.01$) with the two sub-variables *Ethical/Moral* and *Balanced Processing*, compared to no significant correlations with *Self-Awareness* and *Transparency*.

This is particularly interesting, as it means that Self-Compassion could possibly increase a leader's capacity to be guided by his personal values in every situation, especially in those that are morally ambiguous *(Ethical/Moral)*, and to mindfully and empathetically consider different perspectives and consequences of his decisions for everybody involved *(Balanced Processing)*. The very mindful and connecting qualities of Self-Compassion in terms of embracing oneself as part of a larger humanity and to hold one's emotions in balanced awareness could contribute to the development of a balanced ethical consciousness in Authentic Leadership.

On the other hand, Self-Compassion did not significantly correlate with Self-Awareness and Transparency, although it seemed comprehensible that the practice of Self-Compassion in terms of being kind with oneself instead of harshly critical could lead to a higher willingness to deal with one's strengths and limitations openly *(Self-Awareness* and *Transparency)*. We could assume that eventually, a leader with a high sense of Self-Compassion would not necessarily see the need to openly talk about vulnerabilities without directly being asked for it, as he would not need to be in the centre of attention, rather leading in the background, allowing his fellow leaders or followers to be at their best. For further research, the detailed interactions between Self-Compassion and *Self-Awareness* as well as *Transparency* should be examined more closely.

In general, we can see that the relationship between Self-Compassion and Authentic Leadership is more complex than making simple references between parts of Self-Compassion and Authentic Leadership behaviours, looking back to the developed theoretical model earlier on in this publication *(see Fig. 1 in chapter 1.2.3.)*. The development of authenticity can be seen as a major moderating factor between the two constructs, and as definitions of authenticity as a spiritual, psychological or philosophical concept are diverse, the one of most service to effective authentic leading still needs to be formed.

We therefore need to look at two distinct areas separately, as they complement the genesis of Authentic Leadership behaviours: Firstly, it needs to be explored more closely how Self-Compassion exactly contributes to the development of authenticity, and therefore to authentic self-expression in every part of one's being. First investigations about the connection between Self-Compassion, self-esteem and an authentic sense of worthiness were being made by Neff (2003a, 2003b) already, and Brown (2009) sees Self-Compassion as a cornerstone for authentic living on the way out of shame and self-judgment. Second, a commonly agreed on understanding of authenticity needs to be defined in order to be of further use for research about Authentic Leadership and resulting behaviours.

This study further on made a start to understand the influence of independent variables on the relationship between Self-Compassion and Authentic Leadership, such as age, culture, profession or organizational structure. Correlations between Self-Compassion and Authentic Leadership were especially moderate for participants aged less than 30 years, leading or having lead smaller teams with 12 people or less and working for larger organizations with over 1.000 employees. We could for example assume that the correlation was stronger for younger people because they are in an intense phase of their early career. Frequent feedback and self-reflection could lead to a greater awareness of internal attitudes and behaviors, and eventually increase the esteem of authentic development and self-compassionate practices. Especially the so called *'Generation Y'* (see Tulgan, 2009) values self-fulfillment and personal growth more than other generations, which makes individual purpose, happiness and social responsibility common life and career aims.

Furthermore we could hypothesize that the relationship between Self-Compassion and Authentic Leadership becomes more relevant in smaller team settings because interactions are more personal, whereas the value and recognition of Authentic Leadership behaviors in larger team settings is less obvious. On the contrary, this would be inconsistent with the fact that correlations were stronger for people working in large organizations, where bigger sub-teams involving higher levels of anonymity could be expected. We could guess that self-rated compassion and authenticity of leaders in larger organizations is higher because they might have more opportunities to take part in personal development programs. Bigger organizations might face higher pressures to justify their company's work culture to the public, resulting in a strong focus on ethical leadership development.

4.2.2. Practical implications for Authentic Leadership: Self-Compassion as major component for Authentic Leadership Development

Apart from the areas of academic research that are worth exploring in the context of Authentic Leadership and Self-Compassion, several implications for Authentic Leadership in practice derive from this study.

Self-Compassion as a contributing factor for increased authenticity could enrich the depth of Authentic Leadership Development. Especially for the moral component of Authentic Leadership, Self-Compassion could be a major contributing factor. As we have seen in this study, Self-Compassion especially correlated with the *Ethical/Moral* consciousness and *Balanced Processing* of an authentic leader. Contrary to the by May et al. (2003) suggested formal approach of developing a leader's moral capacity using group discussions and reflection of moral dilemmas, the development of Self-Compassion including the acknowledgement of being part of a larger human condition could offer a more effective alternative.

On a holistic level, Self-Compassion could become a major area to support leaders in giving purpose and meaning to their life and organizations. It could support them in dealing mindfully and authentically with their vulnerabilities, weaknesses, and failures, and further on establish a greater sense of worthiness and self-concept clarity. Shamir & Eilam (2005) for example propose that a leader's strong sense of clarity comes from his life story and how he gives meaning to important life events. They say that identity is a story created, told, revised and retold through life, and the connection of different life events forms a meaning system to interpret reality. Now, Interpreting one's own life story from a place of self-compassion and kindness can fundamentally transform the way a leader is identifying with his imperfect self and those around him. It could foster understanding and peace especially with unpleasant life events, and therefore restore integrity and an authentic way of being.

Self-Compassion as a very intimate practice connects well to the statement of Authentic Leadership Development being a deeply personal and life-long learning process that needs to be non-standardized (Avolio & Gardner, 2005; George, 2007). Drawing personal meanings from one's life stories to gain greater clarity about oneself can only happen in a guided reflection process where people return to important life experiences, re-evaluate connected feelings and draw their lessons from it. Individual counselling or small group sessions are seen as most appropriate for this intense and personal process (Shamir & Eilam, 2005), and integrating the variable of Self-Compassion can be highly beneficial. Self-Compassion could especially be valuable to Authentic Leadership Development as it is easier establish compared to a high sense of self-esteem (Neff, 2011). While Self-Compassion offers the same mental health benefits as self-esteem, it involves less focus on self-evaluation, ego-defensiveness, self-enhancement or evaluations based on external sources. The solely kind connection with oneself offers all the benefits needed to sustain a healthy sense of worthiness, especially in times of failure and pain.

Given that Self-Compassion is responsible for a good proportion of a leader's authenticity, Authentic Leadership Development programs would need to include a closer look at the cause for low levels of Self-Compassion, which due to Brown (2005) is rooted in shame. Shame is one of the most primitive and universal human emotions and defined as *'the intensely painful feeling or experience of believing we are flawed and therefore unworthy of love and belonging'* (Brown, 2007, p. 5). It is meant to be a dangerous and destructive force to establish a healthy sense of authenticity, as it leaves people with *'...feelings of fear, blame, disconnection and unworthiness'* (Brown, Hernandez & Villarreal, 2009, p. 357). Human beings would do almost anything to escape that state. In order to establish resilience against shame, psycho-educational group work is being suggested. The 12-week Shame Resilience Curriculum developed by Brown et al. (2009) focuses on creating space for vulnerability amongst the participants, educates participants about shame and its impact on physical and emotional health, explores shame triggers as well as the practice of empathy, and finally leads participants to reach out and establish more authentic, joyful and shame resilient connections with themselves and their surroundings. Training on increasing Self-Compassion can further on be accessed via various Mindfulness centres and research units, offering Mindful Self-Compassion (MSC) programs as well as teacher training (Neff & Germer, 2012).

Following the theory of embodied leadership, Ladkin & Taylor (2010) even argue that the 'true self' of a leader will only be perceived as fully authentic when it is fully embodied. For Authentic Leadership Development, this would mean that the leader needs to balance and resolve paradoxes and tensions originated in bodily and unconscious processes in order to be fully authentic, for example in using theatre techniques. Dealing with old and physically present emotions in one's body would therefore become part of leadership development. It clearly places the leader in a vulnerable place, and the practice of Self-Compassion and self-kindness throughout that journey could be a valuable asset.

5. Recommendations

As we have learnt, the development and practice of Authentic Leadership involves the willingness of deep introspection and confrontation with personal wounds and vulnerabilities. In this sensitive process, the unique qualities of Self-Compassion could contribute tremendously. Both research and practical development of Authentic Leadership would benefit from the integration of Self-Compassion as a major component.

For future research, it would be advisable to examine the qualitative nature of the relationship between Self-Compassion and Authentic Leadership on a more profound level. A qualitative study exploring how authentic leaders relate to themselves in order to identify possible associations with the qualities of Self-Compassion could bring valuable indications. Studies with a bigger sample size investigating potential differences in Self-Compassion and Authentic Leadership between young professionals and experienced leaders, different cultural backgrounds or organizational structures could bring further contextual insights. Self-Compassion could additionally foster the development of a definition of authenticity that is both valid and practical for the further genesis of Authentic Leadership: Self-Compassion connects well with self-related theories grounding the creation of Authentic Leadership characteristics, and it further on can be developed immediately and without large external stimulation, being based on self-kindness and care.

For Authentic Leadership development, Self-Compassion should be considered as an important contributor to this intense and personal process. The acknowledgement of personal vulnerabilities, understanding of one's life story, a greater sense of self-concept clarity, the building of moral capacity as well as compassion for others can all be supported by the practice of Self-Compassion. Authentic Leadership training interventions should consider that the development of authentic and self-expressed individuals is a highly challenging, intense, and rewarding experience. It will confront participants with deep and personal insights about themselves and their surroundings, and an adequate learning environment for this vulnerable process needs to be offered. Shame resilience group-work, psychotherapeutic approaches, embodiment awareness or mindfulness training can be helpful tools to support individuals on their journey.

Authentic self-expression of leaders and followers could finally shape the needed transformation of today's organizations, and even contribute to the progress of humanity. The development of authenticity should be acknowledged as a rewarding, life-long journey, which every human being has the birthright to embark on. The call for authentic being, leading and learning is profoundly necessary and is beautifully manifested in the following:

> *'To the CEOs and teachers. To the principals and the managers.*
> *To the politicians, community leaders, and decision makers:*
>
> *We want to show up, we want to learn, and we want to inspire.*
> *We are hardwired for connection, curiosity, and engagement.*
> *We crave purpose, and we have a deep desire to create and contribute.*
> *We want to take risks, embrace our vulnerabilities, and be courageous.*
>
> *When learning and working are dehumanized – when you no longer see us and no longer encourage our daring, or when you only see what we produce or how we perform – we disengage and turn away from the very things that the world needs from us:*
> *Our talent, our ideas, and our passion.*
>
> *What we ask is that you engage with us, show up beside us, and learn from us.*
> *Feedback is a function of respect; when you don't have honest conversations with us about our strengths and our opportunities for growth, we question our contributions and your commitment.*

Above all else, we ask that you show up, let yourself be seen, and be courageous.

Dare Greatly with us.'

(Brown, 2012, p. 212)

III. References

Avolio, B.J. & Gardner, W.L. (2005). Authentic Leadership Development: Getting to the root of positive forms of leadership. *The Leadership Quaterly,* **16**, 315-338.

Avolio, B.J.; Gardner, W.L.; Walumbwa, F.O.; Luthans, F.; Douglas, R.M. (2004). Unlocking the mask: A look at the process by which authentic leaders impact follower attitudes and behaviors. *The Leadership Quaterly*, **15**, 801 – 823.

Brace, N.; Kemp, R.; Snelgar, R. (2006). SPSS for psychologists. 3rd edition, New York: Palgrave Macmillan.

Brown, B. (2005). Shame resilience theory: A grounded theory study on women and shame. *Families in Society: The Journal of Contemporary Social Services,* **87**, 43–52.

Brown, B. (2007). I thought it was just me: Women reclaiming power and courage in a culture of shame. New York, NY: Penguin Group.

Brown, B.; Hernandez, V.R.; Villarreal, Y. (2009). Connections: A 12-session psychoeducational shame resilience curriculum. In Dearing, R.L. (Ed.) & Tangney, J.P. (Ed.): Shame in the therapy hour, pp. 355 – 371. Washington, DC, US: American Psychological Association.

Brown, B. (2010). The gifts of imperfection: Let go of who you think you're supposed to be and embrace who you are. Minneapolis, MN: Hazelden.

Brown, B. (2012). Daring Greatly: How the Courage to be Vulnerable Transforms the Way we Live, Love, Parent, and Lead. NY, USA: Gotham Books.

Burns, J.M. (1978). Leadership. New York: Harper and Row.

Cranton, P. & Carusetta, E. (2004). Developing Authenticity as a Transformative Process. *Journal of Transformative Education,* **2(4),** 276 – 293.

Diddams, M. & Chang, G.C. (2012). Only human: Exploring the nature of weakness in authentic leadership. *The Leadership Quaterly,* **23**, 593-603.

Gardner, W.L.; Cogliser, C.C.; Davis, K.M.; Dickens, M.P. (2011). Authentic Leadership: A review of the literature and research agenda. *The Leadership Quarterly,* **22**, 1120 – 1145.

Gardner, W.L.; Avolio, B.J.; Walumbwa, F.O. (Eds) (2005). Authentic Leadership Theory and Practice: Origins, Effects and Development. Monographs in Leadership and Management, Volume 3. Bingley, UK: Emerald Group Publishing Limited.

Hall, E.T. (1976). Beyond Culture. New York: Anchor Books.

Ilies, R.; Morgeson, F.P.; Nahrgang, J.D. (2005). Authentic leadership and eudaemonic well-being: Understanding leader-follower outcomes. *The Leadership Quarterly*, **16**, 373 – 394.

Joinson, A. (1999). Social desirability, anonymity, and Internet-based questionnaires. *Behavior Research Methods, Instruments & Computers,* **31(3)**, 433 – 438.

Kernis, M.H. (2003). Toward a Conceptualization of Optimal Self-Esteem. *Psychological Inquiry,* **14 (1),** 1-26.

Kernis, M.H. & Goldman, B.M. (2005): Authenticity: a multicomponent perspective. In Tesster, A., Wood, J., Stapel, D. (Eds.). On Building, Defending, and Regulating the Self: A Psychological Perspective. Psychology Press, New York, 31 – 52.

Kolditz, T.A. & Brazil, D.M. (2005): Authentic Leadership in *In Extremis* settings: A concept for extraordinary leaders in exceptional situations. In Authentic Leadership Theory and Practice: Origins, Effects and Development. *Monographs in Leadership and Management,* **3,** 345 – 356. Bingley, UK: Emerald Group Publishing Limited.

Ladkin, D. & Taylor, S. (2010). Enacting the 'true self': Towards a theory of embodied authentic leadership. *The Leadership Quarterly,* **21,** 64 – 74.

Lakey, C.E.; Kernis, M.H.; Heppner, W.L.; Lance, C.E. (2008). Individual differences in authenticity and mindfulness as predictors of verbal defensiveness. *Journal of Research in Personality,* **42**, 230 – 238.

Leary, M.R.; Tate, E.B.; Allen, A.B.; Adams, C.E.; Hancock, J. (2007). Self-Compassion and Reactions to Unpleasant Self-Relevant Events: The Implications of Treating Oneself Kindly. *Journal of Personality and Social Psychology,* **92(5),** 887 – 904.

Leroy, H.; Palanski, M.E.; Simons, T. (2012). Authentic Leadership and Behavioral Integrity as Drivers of Follower Commitment and Performance. *Journal of Business Ethics,* **107,** 255 – 264.

May, D.R.; Chan, A.Y.; Hodges, T.D.; Avolio, B.J. (2003). Developing the Moral Component of Authentic Leadership. *Organizational Dynamics,* **32(3),** 247 – 260.

Neff, K.D. (2003a). Self-Compassion: An Alternative Conceptualization of a Healthy Attitude Towards Oneself. *Self and Identity,* 2, 85-101.

Neff, K.D. (2003b). The Development and Validation of a Scale to Measure Self-Compassion. *Self and Identity,* 2: 223-250

Neff, K.D.; Kirkpatrick, K.L.; Rude, S.S. (2007a). Self-compassion and adaptive psychological functioning. *Journal of Research in Personality,* **41,** 139 – 154.

Neff, K.D.; Kirkpatrick, K.L.; Rude, S.S. (2007b). An examination of self-compassion in relation to positive psychological functioning and personality traits. *Journal of Research in Personality,* **41,** 908 – 916.

Neff, K.D. & Vonk, R. (2009). Self-Compassion Versus Global Self-Esteem: Two Different Ways of Relating to Oneself. *Journal of Personality,* **77(1),** 23 – 50.

Neff, K.D. (2011). Self-Compassion, Self-Esteem, and Well-Being. *Social and Personality Compass,* **5(1),** 1 – 12.

Neff, K.D. & Beretvas, N. (2013): The Role of Self-Compassion in Romantic Relationships. *Self and Identity,* **12(1),** 78 – 98.

Rego, A.; Sousa, F.; Marques, C.; Pina e Cunha, M. (2012). Authentic leadership promoting employee's psychological capital and creativity. *Journal of Business Research,* **65,** 429-437.

Shamir, B.; Eilam, G. (2005). What's your story? A life-stories approach to authentic leadership development. *The Leadership Quarterly,* **16,** 395 – 417.

Toor, S.-U.-R. & Ofori, G. (2009). Authenticity and its influence on psychological well-being and contingent self-esteem of leaders in Singapore construction sector. *Construction Management and Economics*, **27(3)**, 299 – 313.

Tulgan, B. (2009). Not everyone gets a trophy. How to manage Generation Y. San Francisco, California: Jossey-Bass.

Walumbwa, F. O., Avolio, B. J., Gardner, W. L., Wernsing, T. S., & Peterson, S. J. (2008). Authentic leadership: Development and validation of a theory-based measure. *Journal of Management,* **34,** 89–126.

Wiseman, T. (1996): A concept analysis of empathy. *Journal of Advanced Nursing,* **23,** 1162-1167.

Internet resources:

AIESEC (2013a): Who we are & AIESEC in numbers. https://www.aiesec.org/#/about/mission (date of access 10.08.2013)

AIESEC (2013b): Student opportunities. https://www.aiesec.org/#/learnmore (date of access 16.08.2013)

George, W.W. (2007): True North: Discover your Authentic Leadership. The Raytheon Lectureship in Business Ethics at Bentley College, Center for Business Ethics, Bentley. http://www.billgeorge.org/files/media/true-north-discovering-your-authentic-leadership/GeorgeMonograph.pdf (date of access 25.08.2013)

La Porte, D. (2013): What I know about working with people. Blog entry. http://www.daniellelaporte.com/business-wealth-articles/what-i-know-about-working-with-people-and-yes-this-also-applies-to-romance-as-does-most-business-advice/ (date of access 25.06.2012)

Neff, K.D. & Germer, C.K. (2012). A Pilot Study and Randomized Controlled Trial of the Mindful Self-Compassion Program. http://www.mindfulselfcompassion.org/pdf/Neff%20&%20Germer%20MSC%20RCT%202012.pdf (date of access 20.08.2013).

IV. Appendices

IV.1. Ethics Approval Letter

UNIVERSITY OF FORWARD THINKING WESTMINSTER

Britta Tondock
Student number: 13739407
University of Westminster
Department of Psychology
309 Regent Street
London
W1B 2UW

15 May 2013

Dear Britta

Application Number: PG12/13/230_Psych
Student Name: Britta Tondock

Project title: Does self-compassion increase the level of authenticity of a leader?

I am writing to inform you that your application was considered by the Psychology Ethics Committee. The proposal was **approved**. Please note the conditions below.

Please save this letter as you will be expected to include a hard copy in the appendix section of your project.

Yours sincerely

Debs Harris
Psychology Administrator; School of Social Sciences, Humanities and Languages

---

I am advised by the Committee to remind you of the following points:

1. Please inform your supervisor immediately of any harmful outcomes during the research e.g. participant distress.

2. The need to comply with the Data Protection Act 1998

3. The need to comply, throughout the conduct of the study, with good research practice standards

4. The need to refer proposed amendments to the protocol to the Ethics Committee for further review and to obtain Ethics Committee approval thereto prior to implementation (except only in cases of emergency when the welfare of the subject is paramount).

5. The desirability of including full details of the participant information sheet and consent form in an appendix to your research, and of addressing specifically ethical issues in your methodological discussion.

6 Your responsibility to notify the Ethics Committee immediately of any information received by you, or of which you become aware, which would cast doubt upon, or alter, any information contained in the original application, or a later amendment, submitted to the Ethics Committee and/or which would raise questions about the safety and/or continued conduct of the research.

IV.2. Overview of approached population

Questionnaire posted over 7-week period of time between 13.06.2013 and 01.08.2013 In the following groups on the professional online platforms LinkedIn and XING:

Group name	No. of members on LinkedIn (www.linkedin.com	No. of members on XING (www.xing.de)
Alumni:		
AIESEC Alumni Global	31.764	-
AIESEC Alumni International	2.011	476
AIESEC Alumni Germany	-	4.213
AIESEC Alumni Asia Pacific	1.668	-
AIESEC Africa Alumni network	1.076	-
AIESEC Alumni Brazil	786	-
AIESEC Alumni – Coaching and Training	754	-
AIESEC Alumni UK	361	-
AIESEC MENA Alumni Group	202	-
	38.622	4.689
Active members:		
AIESEC	14.823	
AIESEC Global	-	1.011
	14.832	1.011

IV.3. Measurements

IV.3.1. Questionnaire introduction

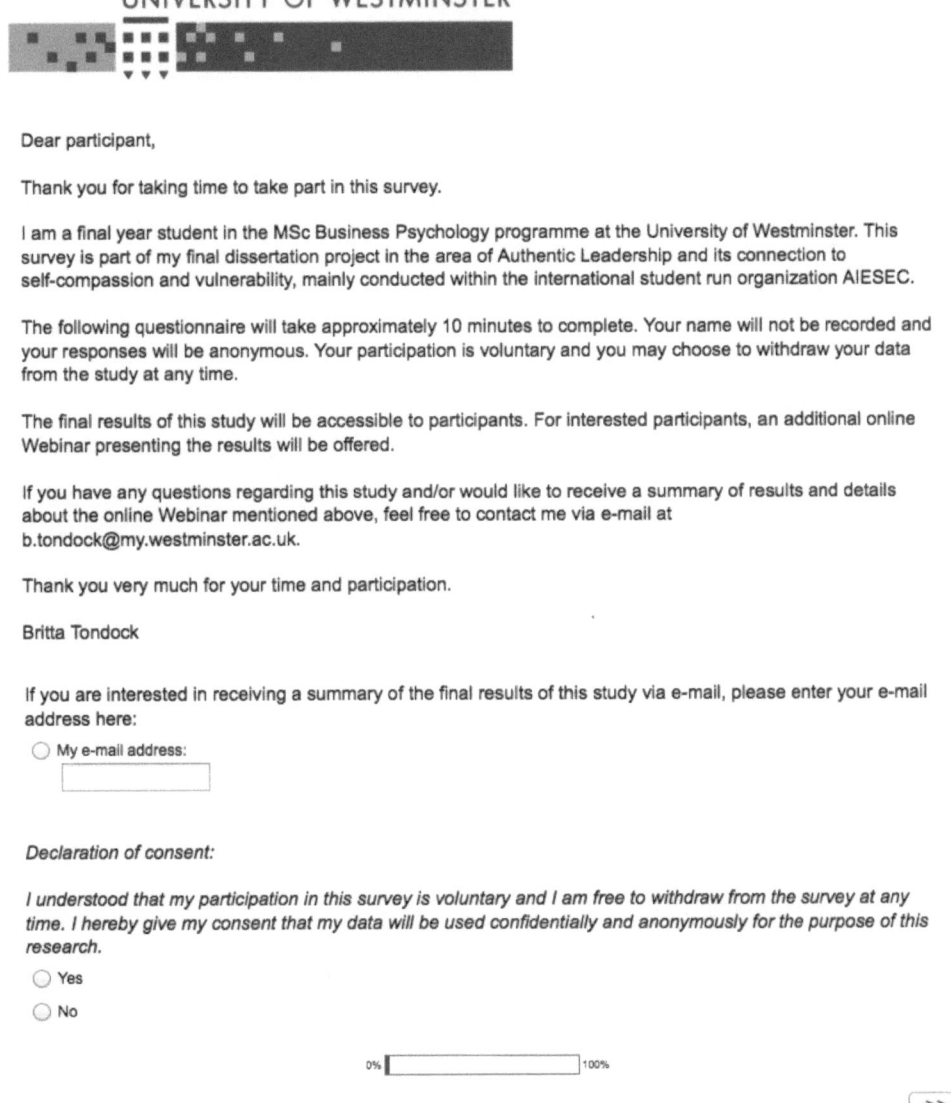

Dear participant,

Thank you for taking time to take part in this survey.

I am a final year student in the MSc Business Psychology programme at the University of Westminster. This survey is part of my final dissertation project in the area of Authentic Leadership and its connection to self-compassion and vulnerability, mainly conducted within the international student run organization AIESEC.

The following questionnaire will take approximately 10 minutes to complete. Your name will not be recorded and your responses will be anonymous. Your participation is voluntary and you may choose to withdraw your data from the study at any time.

The final results of this study will be accessible to participants. For interested participants, an additional online Webinar presenting the results will be offered.

If you have any questions regarding this study and/or would like to receive a summary of results and details about the online Webinar mentioned above, feel free to contact me via e-mail at b.tondock@my.westminster.ac.uk.

Thank you very much for your time and participation.

Britta Tondock

If you are interested in receiving a summary of the final results of this study via e-mail, please enter your e-mail address here:

○ My e-mail address:

Declaration of consent:

I understood that my participation in this survey is voluntary and I am free to withdraw from the survey at any time. I hereby give my consent that my data will be used confidentially and anonymously for the purpose of this research.

○ Yes
○ No

© (2007) Authentic Leadership Questionnaire (ALQ). Bruce J. Avolio, William L. Gardner & Fred O. Walumbwa. Distribution by Mind Garden, Inc. www.mindgarden.com. © (2003) Self-Compassion Scale. Neff, K., University of Texas, Austin, USA.

Survey Powered By Qualtrics

IV.3.2. Demographic questions

UNIVERSITY OF WESTMINSTER

What is your gender?
- ○ Male
- ○ Female

What is your age?
- ○ 18-24 years
- ○ 25-30 years
- ○ 31-35 years
- ○ 36-40 years
- ○ 41-45 years
- ○ 45-50 years
- ○ 51-55 years
- ○ 56-60 years
- ○ 61 and over

What is your highest degree of education?
- ○ High School Diploma or Equivalent
- ○ Associate Degree
- ○ Bachelor of Arts (BA)
- ○ Bachelor of Science (BSc)
- ○ Master of Arts (MA)
- ○ Master of Business Administration (MBA)
- ○ Master of Science (MSc)
- ○ Dr. of Jurisprudence
- ○ Dr. of Medicine (MD)
- ○ Dr. of Philosophy (PhD)
- ○ Other

© (2007) Authentic Leadership Questionnaire (ALQ). Bruce J. Avolio, William L. Gardner & Fred O. Walumbwa. Distribution by Mind Garden, Inc. www.mindgarden.com. © (2003) Self-Compassion Scale. Neff, K., University of Texas, Austin, USA.

Survey Powered By Qualtrics

UNIVERSITY OF WESTMINSTER

What is your current status in AIESEC?
- ○ Active member
- ○ Alumna or Alumnus

Are you currently leading a team or a group of people inside your organization or have you been leading a team or a group of people inside your organization in the past?
- ○ Yes
- ○ No

>>

© (2007) Authentic Leadership Questionnaire (ALQ). Bruce J. Avolio, William L. Gardner & Fred O. Walumbwa. Distribution by Mind Garden, Inc. www.mindgarden.com. © (2003) Self-Compassion Scale. Neff, K., University of Texas, Austin, USA.

Survey Powered By Qualtrics

UNIVERSITY OF WESTMINSTER

How many members does/did your team have?
- ○ 2-5 people
- ○ 6-12 people
- ● 13-20 people
- ○ 21-50 people
- ○ 51-200 people
- ○ 200 and more

>>

© (2007) Authentic Leadership Questionnaire (ALQ). Bruce J. Avolio, William L. Gardner & Fred O. Walumbwa. Distribution by Mind Garden, Inc. www.mindgarden.com. © (2003) Self-Compassion Scale. Neff, K., University of Texas, Austin, USA.

Survey Powered By Qualtrics

UNIVERSITY OF WESTMINSTER

For how many years have you been working in your current/former position?
- ○ 1 year and less
- ○ 2-5 years
- ○ 6-10 years
- ○ 11 years and more

How many people are working for your current/former organization?
- ○ 1-10 employees
- ○ 11-50 employees
- ○ 51-100 employees
- ○ 101-500 employees
- ○ 501-1000 employees
- ○ 1001 employees and more

What is your current geographic region?
- ○ Africa
- ○ Asia
- ○ Central America
- ○ Eastern Europe
- ○ European Union
- ○ Middle East
- ○ Oceania
- ○ South America
- ○ The Caribbean

What is your current area of occupation?

○ Architecture and Engineering Occupations
○ Arts, Design, Entertainment, Sports, and Media Occupations
○ Building and Grounds Cleaning and Maintenance Occupations
○ Business and Financial Operations Occupations
○ Community and Social Service Occupations
○ Computer and Mathematical Occupations
○ Construction and Extraction Occupations
○ Education, Training, and Library Occupations
○ Farming, Fishing and Foresting Occupations
○ Food Preparation and Service Related Occupations
○ Healthcare Practitioners and Technical Occupations
○ Healthcare Support Occupations
○ Installation, Maintenance and Repair Occupations
○ Legal Occupations
○ Life, Physical, and Social Science Occupations
○ Management Occupations
○ Military Specific Occupations
○ Office and Administrative Support Occupations
○ Personal Care and Service Occupations
○ Production Occupations
○ Protective Service Occupations
○ Sales and Related Occupations
○ Transportation and Material Moving Occupations

Please specify briefly what your job role is.

○ My current job role:

0% ▇▇▇▇ 100%

IV.3.3. Authentic Leadership Questionnaire – copyright

www.mindgarden.com

To whom it may concern,

This letter is to grant permission for the above named person to use the following copyright material;

Instrument: Authentic Leadership Questionnaire (ALQ)

Authors: Bruce J. Avolio, William L. Gardner, and Fred O. Walumbwa

Copyright: "Copyright © 2007 Authentic Leadership Questionnaire (ALQ) by Bruce J. Avolio, William L. Gardner, and Fred O. Walumbwa. All rights reserved in all medium."

for his/her thesis research.
 Three sample items from this instrument may be reproduced for inclusion in a proposal, thesis, or dissertation.

The entire instrument may not be included or reproduced at any time in any other published material.

Sincerely,

Robert Most
Mind Garden, Inc.
www.mindgarden.com

IV.3.4. Authentic Leadership Questionnaire – online terms of use

Source: *http://www.mindgarden.com/how.htm#instrumentweb (date of access 10.08.2013)*

Using an Outside Survey Website

We understand that sometimes it is necessary or desirable to put an instrument on an outside survey website for data collection, and in this case you will need to take two steps:

1) Purchase a License to Use the instrument in the form of PDF, in an amount equal to or greater than the number you intend to use. (PDF licenses are generally for data collection for research only; if you require commercial use please contact Mind Garden).

2) Complete a short Online Use application to insure that you understand how to properly protect the Mind Garden instrument.

Please note that NOT ALL of our instruments may be put on the web (The drop-down menu on our online agreement form contains a complete list of instruments that may be put online).

DISTRIBUTING AN ENTIRE INSTRUMENT IN EITHER THE TEXT OF AN EMAIL OR AS AN EMAIL ATTACHMENT IS STRICTLY PROHIBITED.

After your purchase of a Reproduction License, please complete our Online Use form (See link below). Before you get started, you'll need your order number as a reference.

- Your name and institution
- The title of your research project
- The name of the Mind Garden instrument (via drop down menu)
- Your Mind Garden invoice number or sales receipt number.
- A statement that:
    - ...you have compensated Mind Garden for the appropriate number of reproductions and will compensate Mind Garden for every administration of the online survey. Note: An administration or license is considered "used" when a respondent **views** one or more items/questions, regardless of whether the respondent completes the survey.
    - ...you will put the instrument copyright (including www.mindgarden.com) on every page containing questions/items from this instrument.
    - ...you will remove your survey from the internet/survey site at the conclusion of your data collection.
    - ...your survey will not be on the "open web". **Ideal research practice involves knowing who is responding to your survey, although this is not always possible. We recommend, but do not require, a unique login and password for every respondent.** *CAUTION: If you decide not to require a unique login for each respondent, the survey method you use* **may** *elicit a large number of responses to your survey. If the response count gets out of your control, YOU are responsible for compensating Mind Garden for every administration, regardless of circumstances.*
    - Please specify the outside online survey website that you will be using.
    - IMPORTANT NOTE: **You may NOT send Mind Garden instruments in the text of an email or as a PDF file to participants.**

IV.3.5. Self-Compassion Scale

HOW I TYPICALLY ACT TOWARDS MYSELF IN DIFFICULT TIMES

Please read each statement carefully before answering. To the left of each item, indicate how often you behave in the stated manner, using the following scale:

Almost never				Almost always
1	2	3	4	5

_____ 1. I'm disapproving and judgmental about my own flaws and inadequacies.

_____ 2. When I'm feeling down I tend to obsess and fixate on everything that's wrong.

_____ 3. When things are going badly for me, I see the difficulties as part of life that everyone goes through.

_____ 4. When I think about my inadequacies, it tends to make me feel more separate and cut off from the rest of the world.

_____ 5. I try to be loving towards myself when I'm feeling emotional pain.

_____ 6. When I fail at something important to me I become consumed by feelings of inadequacy.

_____ 7. When I'm down and out, I remind myself that there are lots of other people in the world feeling like I am.

_____ 8. When times are really difficult, I tend to be tough on myself.

_____ 9. When something upsets me I try to keep my emotions in balance.

_____ 10. When I feel inadequate in some way, I try to remind myself that feelings of inadequacy are shared by most people.

_____ 11. I'm intolerant and impatient towards those aspects of my personality I don't like.

_____ 12. When I'm going through a very hard time, I give myself the caring and tenderness I need.

_____ 13. When I'm feeling down, I tend to feel like most other people are probably happier than I am.

_____ 14. When something painful happens I try to take a balanced view of the situation.

_____ 15. I try to see my failings as part of the human condition.

_____ 16. When I see aspects of myself that I don't like, I get down on myself.

_____ 17. When I fail at something important to me I try to keep things in perspective.

_____ 18. When I'm really struggling, I tend to feel like other people must be having an easier time of it.

_____ 19. I'm kind to myself when I'm experiencing suffering.

_____ 20. When something upsets me I get carried away with my feelings.

_____ 21. I can be a bit cold-hearted towards myself when I'm experiencing suffering.

_____ 22. When I'm feeling down I try to approach my feelings with curiosity and openness.

_____ 23. I'm tolerant of my own flaws and inadequacies.

_____ 24. When something painful happens I tend to blow the incident out of proportion.

_____ 25. When I fail at something that's important to me, I tend to feel alone in my failure.

_____ 26. I try to be understanding and patient towards those aspects of my personality I don't like.

To all interested, please feel free to use the Self-Compassion Scale for research or use with any other population. It is appropriate for ages 14 and up (as long as individuals have at lease an 8th grade reading level). If you aren't that interested in using the subscales, you might also want to consider using the Short SCS (12 items), which has a near perfect correlation with the long scale.

Coding Key:
Self-Kindness Items: 5, 12, 19, 23, 26
Self-Judgment Items: 1, 8, 11, 16, 21
Common Humanity Items: 3, 7, 10, 15
Isolation Items: 4, 13, 18, 25
Mindfulness Items: 9, 14, 17, 22
Over-identified Items: 2, 6, 20, 24

Subscale scores are computed by calculating the mean of subscale item responses. To compute a total self-compassion score, reverse score the negative subscale items - self-judgment, isolation, and over-identification (i.e., 1 = 5, 2 = 4, 3 = 3. 4 = 2, 5 = 1) - then compute a total mean.

IV.4. Sample characteristics

IV.4.1. Overview about demographic data

N = 50									
1. Gender	Male				Female				
	25 *(50 %)*				25 *(50%)*				
2. Age in years	18-24	25-30	31-35	36-40	41-45	45-50	51-55	56-60	>60
	11 *(22%)*	24 *(48%)*	5 *(10%)*	4 *(8%)*	2 *(4%)*	1 *(2%)*	1 *(2%)*	-	2 *(4%)*
3. Geographic Region	EU	South America	Asia	Africa	Central America	Oceania	Eastern Europe	Middle East	The Caribbean
	36 *(72%)*	5 *(10%)*	3 *(6%)*	4 *(8%)*	1 *(2%)*	1 *(2%)*	-	-	-
4. Educational background	MBA	MA	MSc	BSc	BA	High School Diploma	Associate Degree	Other	Dr./PhD

		10 (20%)	8 (16%)	6 (12%)	9 (18%)	5 (10%)	7 (14%)	2 (4%)	3 (6%)	-
5. Status in AIESEC		Alumni				Active				
		42 (84%)				8 (16%)				
6. Number of team members		2-5	6-12	13-20	21-50	51-200	>200			
		14 (28%)	20 (40%)	5 (10%)	6 (12%)	4 (8%)	1 (2%)			
7. Number of years of LS experience		<1	2-5	6-10	>11					
		20 (40%)	25 (50%)	4 (8%)	1 (2%)					
8. Company size (No. of people)		1-10	11-50	51-100	101-500	501-1000	>1001			
		9 (18%)	10 (20%)	10 (20%)	7 (14%)	2 (4%)	12 (24%)			
9. Area of occupation (incl. free text box to specify)	Education, Training and Library Occupations				15 (30%)	Trainer, teacher, facilitator, education assistant, freelancer, social worker, coach, business developer, consultant, key account manager, language trainer, leadership consultant, director, employee engagement				
	Management Occupations				8 (16%)	Partner and head of country division, facilitator and trainer, project manager, head of HR, exchange manager for trainees, management consultant, Vice President Talent Management, coach and company developer				
	Business and Financial Occupations				5 (10%)	CFO, CPO, WFO, consultant global mobility, revenue management specialist				
	Sales and Related Occupations				4 (8%)	Business manager, online marketing, intern public relations and public affairs, regional sales manager				
	Architecture and Engineering Occupations				5 (10%)	Student, undergraduate, national support team incoming exchange and external				

			relations, civil engineer
	Life, Physical and Social Sciences Occupations	3 (6%)	Economics student, policy analyst, anthropology and economics,
	Community and Social Service Occupations	2 (4%)	Project leader, project coordinator
	Personal Care and Service Occupations	2 (4%)	Human resource tasks, marketing and consumer goods and personal care
	Farming, Fishing and Foresting Occupations	1 (2%)	Senior in managing farming
	Computer and Mathematical Occupations	1 (2%)	Head of IS
	Construction and Extraction Occupations	1 (2%)	Assistant engineer
	Healthcare Practitioners and Technical Occupations	1 (2%)	Student
	Arts, Design, Entertainment, Sports and Media Occupations	1 (2%)	Team leader
	Office and Administrative Occupations	1 (2%)	Senior HR advisor
	Building, Grounds Cleaning and Maintenance Occupations	-	
	Food Preparation and Service Related Occupations	-	
	Healthcare Support Occupations	-	
	Installation, Maintenance and Repair Occupations	-	
	Legal Occupations	-	
	Military Specific Occupations	-	
	Production Occupations	-	
	Protective Service Occupations	-	
	Transportation and Material Moving Occupations	-	

IV.4.2. Age distribution

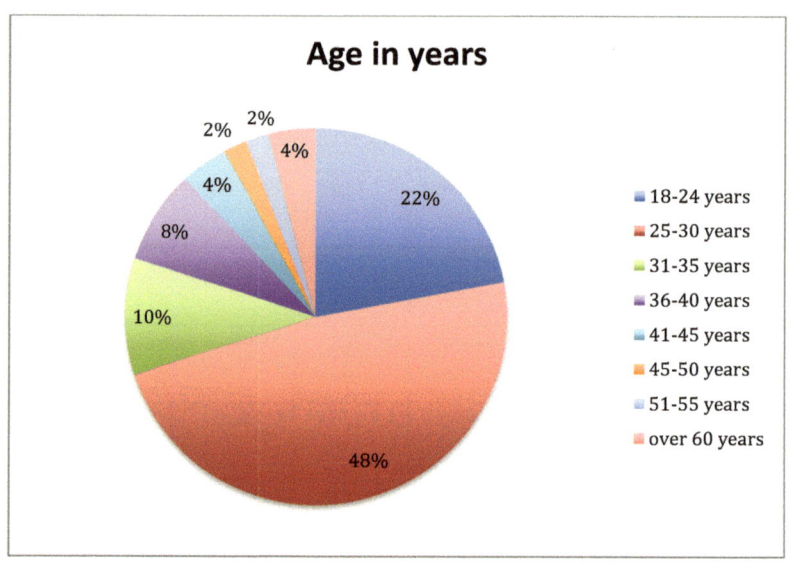

IV.4.3. Geographic Region

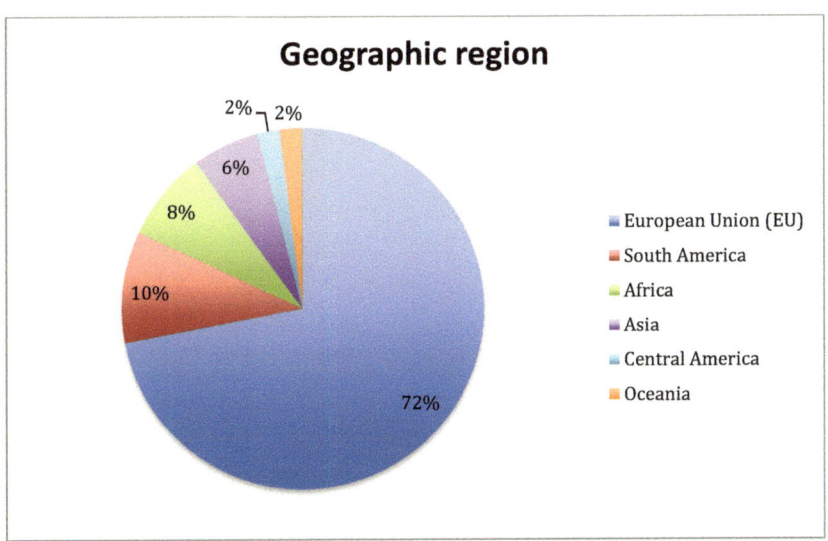

IV.4.4. Educational background

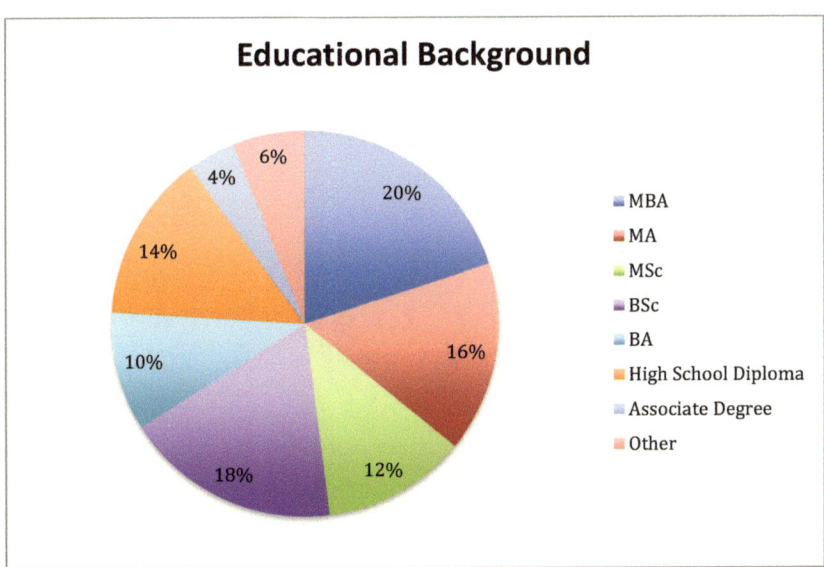

IV.4.5. Number of team members

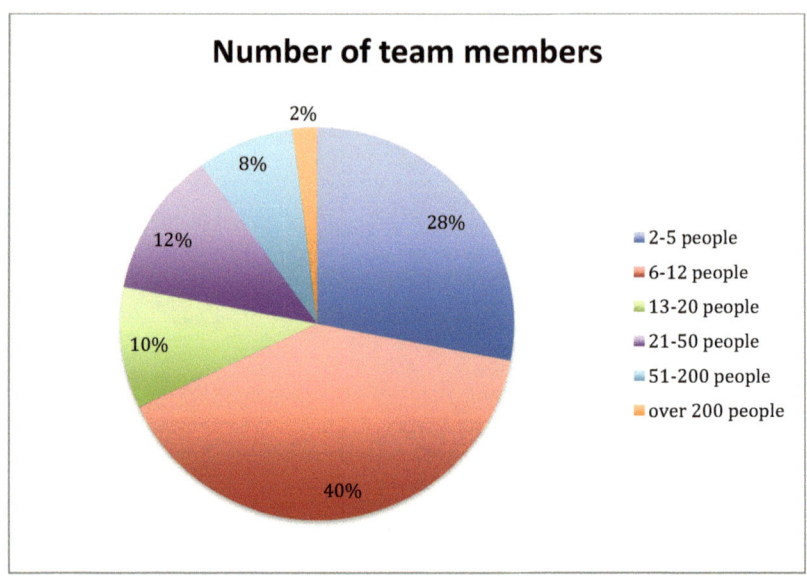

IV.4.6. Leadership experience in years

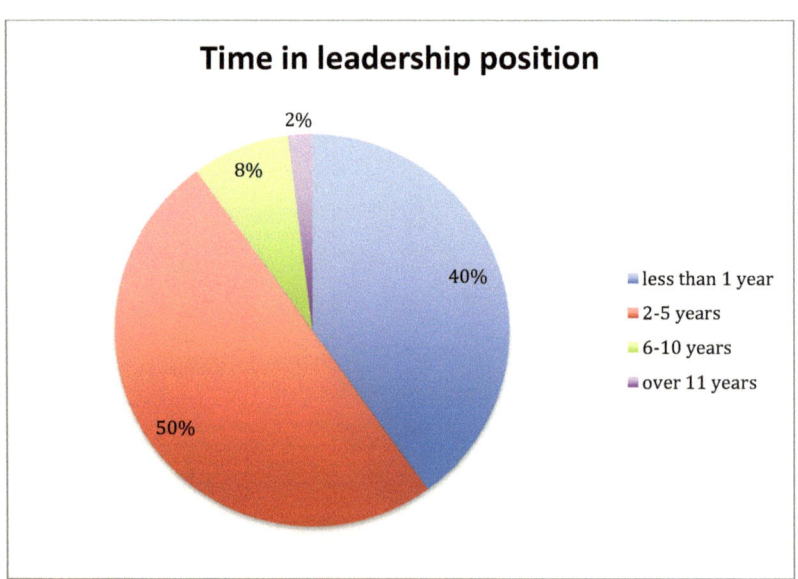

IV.4.7. Size of organization

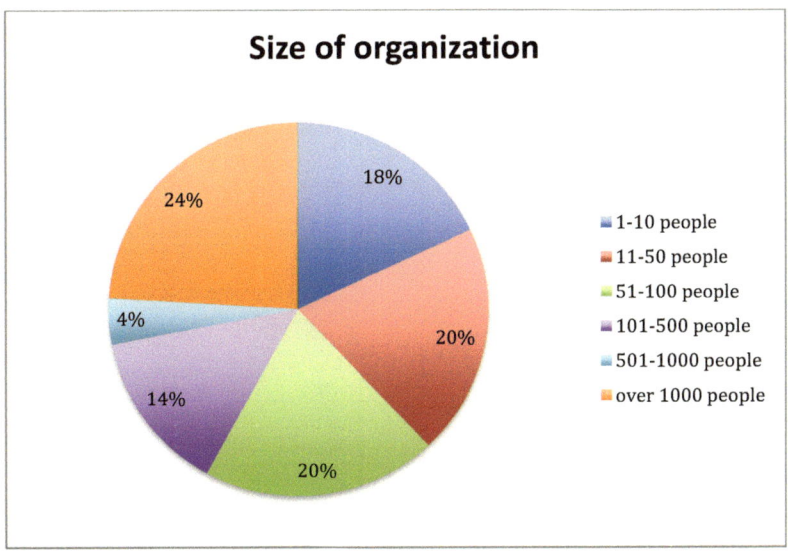

IV.4.8. Occupational background

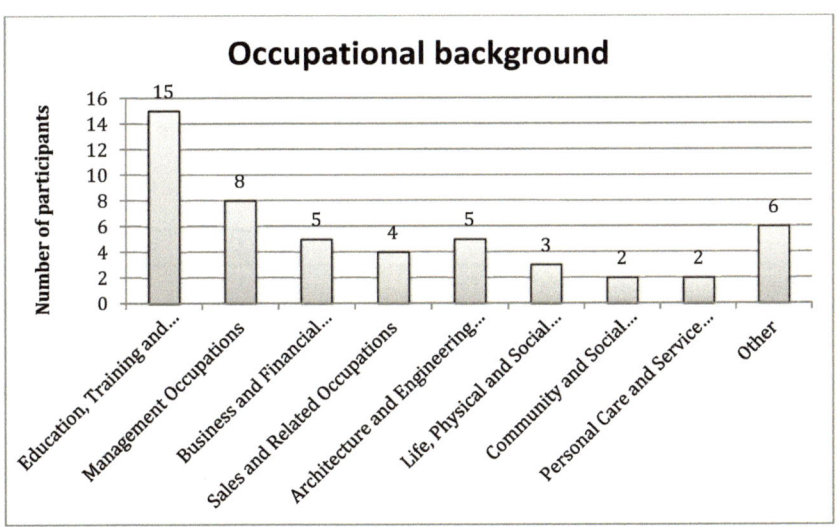

IV.5. Statistical analysis

IV.5.1. Descriptive graphs

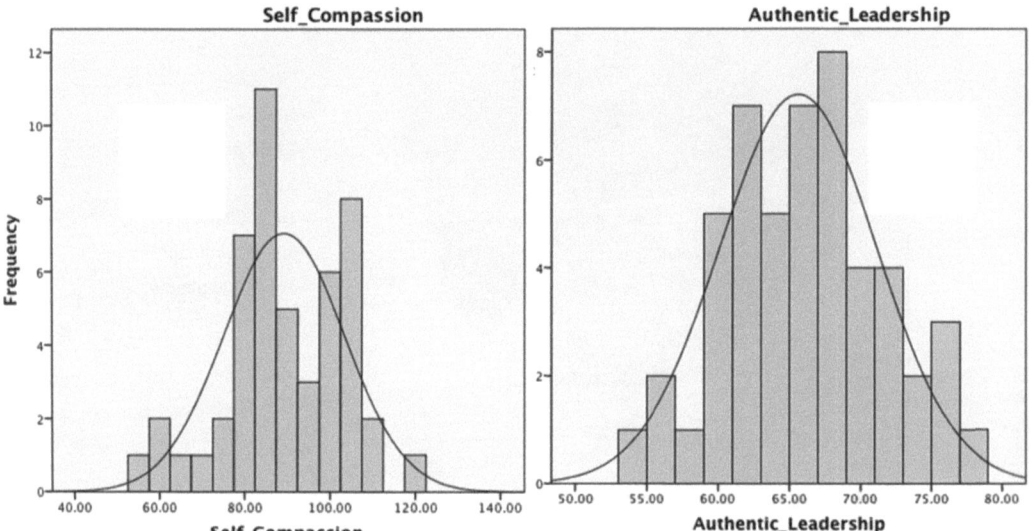

IV.5.2. Inferential analysis of the data

IV.5.2.1. Correlation: Self-Compassion and Authentic Leadership

Descriptive Statistics

	N	Minimum	Maximum	Mean	Std. Deviation	Variance
Self_Compassion	50	55.00	121.00	89.2400	14.14006	199.941
Authentic_Leadership	50	54.00	78.00	65.6200	5.52874	30.567
Valid N (listwise)	50					

Correlations

		Self_Compassion	Authentic_Leadership
Self_Compassion	Pearson Correlation	1	.279[*]
	Sig. (1-tailed)		.025
	N	50	50

		Pearson Correlation	.279*	1
Authentic_Leadership		Sig. (1-tailed)	.025	
		N	50	50

*. Correlation is significant at the 0.05 level (1-tailed).

IV.5.2.2. Correlation: Self-Kindness and Ethical/Moral

Descriptive Statistics

	Mean	Std. Deviation	N
Self_Kindness	32.5400	5.53729	50
Ethial_Moral	16.8000	1.81827	50

Correlations

		Self_Kindness	Ethial_Moral
Self_Kindness	Pearson Correlation	1	.335**
	Sig. (1-tailed)		.009
	N	50	50
Ethial_Moral	Pearson Correlation	.335**	1
	Sig. (1-tailed)	.009	
	N	50	50

**. Correlation is significant at the 0.01 level (1-tailed).

IV.5.2.3. Correlation: Self-Kindness and Balanced Processing

Descriptive Statistics

	Mean	Std. Deviation	N
Self_Kindness	32.5400	5.53729	50
Balanced_Processing	12.2800	1.48516	50

Correlations

		Self_Kindness	Balanced_Processing
Self_Kindness	Pearson Correlation	1	.289*
	Sig. (1-tailed)		.021
	N	50	50
Balanced_Processing	Pearson Correlation	.289*	1
	Sig. (1-tailed)	.021	
	N	50	50

*. Correlation is significant at the 0.05 level (1-tailed).

IV.5.2.4. Correlation: Common Humanity and Ethical/Moral

Descriptive Statistics

	Mean	Std. Deviation	N
Common_Humanity	28.1000	5.61430	50
Ethial_Moral	16.8000	1.81827	50

Correlations

		Common_Humanity	Ethial_Moral
Common_Humanity	Pearson Correlation	1	.282*
	Sig. (1-tailed)		.024
	N	50	50
Ethial_Moral	Pearson Correlation	.282*	1
	Sig. (1-tailed)	.024	
	N	50	50

*. Correlation is significant at the 0.05 level (1-tailed).

IV.5.2.5. Correlation: Common Humanity and Balanced Processing

Descriptive Statistics

	Mean	Std. Deviation	N
Common_Humanity	28.1000	5.61430	50
Balanced_Processing	12.2800	1.48516	50

Correlations

		Common_Humanity	Balanced_Processing
Common_Humanity	Pearson Correlation	1	.271*
	Sig. (1-tailed)		.029
	N	50	50
Balanced_Processing	Pearson Correlation	.271*	1
	Sig. (1-tailed)	.029	
	N	50	50

*. Correlation is significant at the 0.05 level (1-tailed).

IV.5.2.6. Correlation: Mindfulness and Ethical/Moral

Descriptive Statistics

	Mean	Std. Deviation	N
Mindfulness	28.6000	4.82341	50
Ethial_Moral	16.8000	1.81827	50

Correlations

		Mindfulness	Ethial_Moral
Mindfulness	Pearson Correlation	1	.330**
	Sig. (1-tailed)		.010
	N	50	50
Ethial_Moral	Pearson Correlation	.330**	1
	Sig. (1-tailed)	.010	
	N	50	50

**. Correlation is significant at the 0.01 level (1-tailed).

IV.5.2.7. Correlation: Mindfulness and Balanced Processing

Descriptive Statistics

	Mean	Std. Deviation	N
Mindfulness	28.6000	4.82341	50
Balanced_Processing	12.2800	1.48516	50

Correlations

		Mindfulness	Balanced_Processing
Mindfulness	Pearson Correlation	1	.335**
	Sig. (1-tailed)		.009
	N	50	50
Balanced_Processing	Pearson Correlation	.335**	1
	Sig. (1-tailed)	.009	
	N	50	50

**. Correlation is significant at the 0.01 level (1-tailed).

IV.5.2.8. Correlation: Self-Compassion and Ethical/Moral

Descriptive Statistics

	Mean	Std. Deviation	N
Self_Compassion	89.2400	14.14006	50
Ethial_Moral	16.8000	1.81827	50

Correlations

		Self_Compassion	Ethial_Moral
Self_Compassion	Pearson Correlation	1	.356**
	Sig. (1-tailed)		.006
	N	50	50
Ethial_Moral	Pearson Correlation	.356**	1
	Sig. (1-tailed)	.006	
	N	50	50

**. Correlation is significant at the 0.01 level (1-tailed).

IV.5.2.9. Correlation: Self-Compassion and Balanced Processing

Descriptive Statistics

	Mean	Std. Deviation	N
Self_Compassion	89.2400	14.14006	50
Balanced_Processing	12.2800	1.48516	50

Correlations

		Self_Compassion	Balanced_Processing
Self_Compassion	Pearson Correlation	1	.335**
	Sig. (1-tailed)		.009
	N	50	50
Balanced_Processing	Pearson Correlation	.335**	1
	Sig. (1-tailed)	.009	
	N	50	50

**. Correlation is significant at the 0.01 level (1-tailed).

IV.5.2.10. Correlation: Authentic Leadership and Common Humanity

Descriptive Statistics

	Mean	Std. Deviation	N
Authentic_Leadership	65.6200	5.52874	50
Common_Humanity	28.1000	5.61430	50

Correlations

		Authentic_Leadership	Common_Humanity
Authentic_Leadership	Pearson Correlation	1	.249*
	Sig. (1-tailed)		.041
	N	50	50
Common_Humanity	Pearson Correlation	.249*	1
	Sig. (1-tailed)	.041	
	N	50	50

*. Correlation is significant at the 0.05 level (1-tailed).

IV.5.2.11. Correlation: Authentic Leadership and Mindfulness

Descriptive Statistics

	Mean	Std. Deviation	N
Authentic_Leadership	65.6200	5.52874	50
Mindfulness	28.6000	4.82341	50

Correlations

		Authentic_Leadership	Mindfulness
Authentic_Leadership	Pearson Correlation	1	.266*
	Sig. (1-tailed)		.031
	N	50	50
Mindfulness	Pearson Correlation	.266*	1
	Sig. (1-tailed)	.031	
	N	50	50

*. Correlation is significant at the 0.05 level (1-tailed).

IV.5.3. Correlations for different sub-groups

IV.5.3.1. Overview

Strength of correlation in different subgroups			
1. Gender	Male	Female	
	.243 (N=25)	.324 (N=25)	
2. Age	<30 years	>30 years	
	.300* (N=35)	.201 (N=15)	
3. Status in AIESEC	Active	Alumni	
	.706* (N=8)	.246 (N=42)	
4. Team size	<13 people	>13 people	
	.326* (N=34)	.072 (N=16)	
5. Leadership XP	>1 year	2-5 years	>5 years
	.258 (N=20)	.320 (N=25)	.581 (N=5)
6. Company size	<100 people	>100 people	
	.205 (N=29)	.414* (N=21)	
7. Geographic region	EU	South America	Asia
	.354* (N=36)	-.278 (N=5)	.727 (N=4)
5. Occupation	Education & Training	Management (N=8)	Business & Financial
	.358 (N=15)	-.128 (N=8)	.867* (N=5)

IV.5.3.2. Male sample

Descriptive Statistics

	Mean	Std. Deviation	N
Self_Compassion	89.4800	12.07656	25
Authentic_Leadership	64.6000	5.42371	25

Correlations

		Self_Compassion	Authentic_Leadership
Self_Compassion	Pearson Correlation	1	.243
	Sig. (1-tailed)		.121
	N	25	25
Authentic_Leadership	Pearson Correlation	.243	1
	Sig. (1-tailed)	.121	
	N	25	25

IV.5.3.3. Female sample

Descriptive Statistics

	Mean	Std. Deviation	N
Self_Compassion	89.0000	16.19413	25
Authentic_Leadership	66.6400	5.55188	25

Correlations

		Self_Compassion	Authentic_Leadership
Self_Compassion	Pearson Correlation	1	.324
	Sig. (1-tailed)		.057
	N	25	25
Authentic_Leadership	Pearson Correlation	.324	1
	Sig. (1-tailed)	.057	
	N	25	25

IV.5.3.4. Age less than 30 years

Descriptive Statistics

	Mean	Std. Deviation	N
Self_Compassion	88.9143	14.83313	35
Authentic_Leadership	64.8000	5.61406	35

Correlations

		Self_Compassion	Authentic_Leadership
Self_Compassion	Pearson Correlation	1	.300*
	Sig. (1-tailed)		.040
	N	35	35
Authentic_Leadership	Pearson Correlation	.300*	1
	Sig. (1-tailed)	.040	
	N	35	35

*. Correlation is significant at the 0.05 level (1-tailed).

IV.5.3.5. Age more than 30 years

Descriptive Statistics

	Mean	Std. Deviation	N
Self_Compassion	90.0000	12.82854	15
Authentic_Leadership	67.5333	4.98378	15

Correlations

		Self_Compassion	Authentic_Leadership
Self_Compassion	Pearson Correlation	1	.210
	Sig. (1-tailed)		.226
	N	15	15
Authentic_Leadership	Pearson Correlation	.210	1
	Sig. (1-tailed)	.226	
	N	15	15

IV.5.3.6. Active AIESECers

Descriptive Statistics

	Mean	Std. Deviation	N
Self_Compassion	91.5000	10.73046	8
Authentic_Leadership	63.8750	5.19443	8

Correlations

		Self_Compassion	Authentic_Leadership
Self_Compassion	Pearson Correlation	1	.706*
	Sig. (1-tailed)		.025
	N	8	8
Authentic_Leadership	Pearson Correlation	.706*	1
	Sig. (1-tailed)	.025	
	N	8	8

*. Correlation is significant at the 0.05 level (1-tailed).

IV.5.3.7. Alumni

Descriptive Statistics

	Mean	Std. Deviation	N
Self_Compassion	88.8095	14.76852	42
Authentic_Leadership	65.9524	5.58723	42

Correlations

		Self_Compassion	Authentic_Leadership
Self_Compassion	Pearson Correlation	1	.246
	Sig. (1-tailed)		.058
	N	42	42
Authentic_Leadership	Pearson Correlation	.246	1
	Sig. (1-tailed)	.058	
	N	42	42

IV.5.3.8. Team size 2-12 people

Descriptive Statistics

	Mean	Std. Deviation	N
Self_Compassion	88.8235	16.11788	34
Authentic_Leadership	66.3529	6.16875	34

Correlations

		Self_Compassion	Authentic_Leadership
Self_Compassion	Pearson Correlation	1	.326[*]
	Sig. (1-tailed)		.030
	N	34	34
Authentic_Leadership	Pearson Correlation	.326[*]	1
	Sig. (1-tailed)	.030	
	N	34	34

*. Correlation is significant at the 0.05 level (1-tailed).

IV.5.3.9. Team size over 12 people

Descriptive Statistics

	Mean	Std. Deviation	N
Self_Compassion	90.1250	8.96568	16
Authentic_Leadership	64.0625	3.51129	16

Correlations

		Self_Compassion	Authentic_Leadership
Self_Compassion	Pearson Correlation	1	.072
	Sig. (1-tailed)		.396
	N	16	16
Authentic_Leadership	Pearson Correlation	.072	1
	Sig. (1-tailed)	.396	
	N	16	16

IV.5.3.10. Less than 1 year of leadership experience

Descriptive Statistics

	Mean	Std. Deviation	N
Self_Compassion	91.6500	12.06681	20
Authentic_Leadership	65.1000	6.30706	20

Correlations

		Self_Compassion	Authentic_Leadership
Self_Compassion	Pearson Correlation	1	.258
	Sig. (1-tailed)		.136
	N	20	20
Authentic_Leadership	Pearson Correlation	.258	1
	Sig. (1-tailed)	.136	
	N	20	20

IV.5.3.11. 2-5 years of leadership experience

Descriptive Statistics

	Mean	Std. Deviation	N
Self_Compassion	87.8000	15.25615	25
Authentic_Leadership	65.4000	5.12348	25

Correlations

		Self_Compassion	Authentic_Leadership
Self_Compassion	Pearson Correlation	1	.320
	Sig. (1-tailed)		.060
	N	25	25
Authentic_Leadership	Pearson Correlation	.320	1
	Sig. (1-tailed)	.060	
	N	25	25

IV.5.3.12. Over 5 years of leadership experience

Descriptive Statistics

	Mean	Std. Deviation	N
Self_Compassion	86.8000	17.65503	5
Authentic_Leadership	68.8000	3.70135	5

Correlations

		Self_Compassion	Authentic_Leadership
Self_Compassion	Pearson Correlation	1	.581
	Sig. (1-tailed)		.152
	N	5	5
Authentic_Leadership	Pearson Correlation	.581	1
	Sig. (1-tailed)	.152	
	N	5	5

IV.5.3.13. Company size 1-100 people

Descriptive Statistics

	Mean	Std. Deviation	N
Self_Compassion	88.0345	14.17614	29
Authentic_Leadership	65.8966	5.77770	29

Correlations

		Self_Compassion	Authentic_Leadership
Self_Compassion	Pearson Correlation	1	.205
	Sig. (1-tailed)		.144
	N	29	29
Authentic_Leadership	Pearson Correlation	.205	1
	Sig. (1-tailed)	.144	
	N	29	29

IV.5.3.14. Company size over 100 people

Descriptive Statistics

	Mean	Std. Deviation	N
Self_Compassion	90.9048	14.26501	21
Authentic_Leadership	65.2381	5.28114	21

Correlations

		Self_Compassion	Authentic_Leadership
Self_Compassion	Pearson Correlation	1	.414*
	Sig. (1-tailed)		.031
	N	21	21
Authentic_Leadership	Pearson Correlation	.414*	1
	Sig. (1-tailed)	.031	
	N	21	21

*. Correlation is significant at the 0.05 level (1-tailed).

IV.5.3.15. European Union

Descriptive Statistics

	Mean	Std. Deviation	N
Self_Compassion	89.3333	14.74158	36
Authentic_Leadership	65.9722	5.18507	36

Correlations

		Self_Compassion	Authentic_Leadership
Self_Compassion	Pearson Correlation	1	.354[*]
	Sig. (1-tailed)		.017
	N	36	36
Authentic_Leadership	Pearson Correlation	.354[*]	1
	Sig. (1-tailed)	.017	
	N	36	36

*. Correlation is significant at the 0.05 level (1-tailed).

IV.5.3.16. South America

Descriptive Statistics

	Mean	Std. Deviation	N
Self_Compassion	94.0000	10.09950	5
Authentic_Leadership	63.4000	3.91152	5

Correlations

		Self_Compassion	Authentic_Leadership
Self_Compassion	Pearson Correlation	1	-.278
	Sig. (1-tailed)		.325
	N	5	5
Authentic_Leadership	Pearson Correlation	-.278	1
	Sig. (1-tailed)	.325	
	N	5	5

IV.5.3.17. Africa

Descriptive Statistics

	Mean	Std. Deviation	N
Self_Compassion	74.6667	12.74101	3
Authentic_Leadership	70.6667	5.50757	3

Correlations

		Self_Compassion	Authentic_Leadership
Self_Compassion	Pearson Correlation	1	.924
	Sig. (1-tailed)		.125
	N	3	3
Authentic_Leadership	Pearson Correlation	.924	1
	Sig. (1-tailed)	.125	
	N	3	3

IV.5.3.18. Asia

Descriptive Statistics

	Mean	Std. Deviation	N
Self_Compassion	87.7500	9.39415	4
Authentic_Leadership	61.5000	5.19615	4

Correlations

		Self_Compassion	Authentic_Leadership
Self_Compassion	Pearson Correlation	1	.727
	Sig. (1-tailed)		.136
	N	4	4
Authentic_Leadership	Pearson Correlation	.727	1
	Sig. (1-tailed)	.136	
	N	4	4

IV.5.3.19. Education & Training occupations

Descriptive Statistics

	Mean	Std. Deviation	N
Self_Compassion	86.4667	16.90675	15
Authentic_Leadership	65.5333	4.73387	15

Correlations

		Self_Compassion	Authentic_Leadership
Self_Compassion	Pearson Correlation	1	.358
	Sig. (1-tailed)		.095
	N	15	15
Authentic_Leadership	Pearson Correlation	.358	1
	Sig. (1-tailed)	.095	
	N	15	15

IV.5.3.20. Management occupations

Descriptive Statistics

	Mean	Std. Deviation	N
Self_Compassion	89.1250	10.94711	8
Authentic_Leadership	65.3750	5.52753	8

Correlations

		Self_Compassion	Authentic_Leadership
Self_Compassion	Pearson Correlation	1	-.128
	Sig. (1-tailed)		.381
	N	8	8
Authentic_Leadership	Pearson Correlation	-.128	1
	Sig. (1-tailed)	.381	
	N	8	8

IV.5.3.21. Business & Financial occupations

Descriptive Statistics

	Mean	Std. Deviation	N
Self_Compassion	94.0000	19.40361	5
Authentic_Leadership	66.4000	7.70065	5

Correlations

		Self_Compassion	Authentic_Leadership
Self_Compassion	Pearson Correlation	1	.867[*]
	Sig. (1-tailed)		.029
	N	5	5
Authentic_Leadership	Pearson Correlation	.867[*]	1
	Sig. (1-tailed)	.029	
	N	5	5

*. Correlation is significant at the 0.05 level (1-tailed).